W9-AJO-659

THE
ENCYCLOPEDIA
OF WAR&
WEAPONRY

WARS OF CHARLEMAGNE In the 9th century, a Frankish army led by Charlemagne conquers a city. This is a 14th century illustration of the battle.

THE
ENCYCLOPEDIA
OF WAR&
WEAPONRY

STUART MURRAY

Franklin Watts
A Division of Scholastic Inc.
New York   Toronto   London   Auckland   Sydney
Mexico City   New Delhi   Hong Kong

Danbury, Connecticut

CREATED IN ASSOCIATION WITH MEDIA PROJECTS INCORPORATED
C. Carter Smith, Executive Editor
Carter Smith III, Managing Editor
Aaron Murray, Project Editor
Ron Toelke, Consulting Editor
Ron Toelke Associates, Graphic Design

FRANKLIN WATTS STAFF
Phil Friedman, Publishing Director
Andrew Hudak, Editor
Marie O'Neill, Art Director

TITLE PAGE ILLUSTRATION
Page 2: 14th century illustration, from a French illuminated manuscript, SuperStock.
Page 3: presentation of mid-19th century arms and equipment, courtesy Ron Toelke,
The Complete Encyclopedia of Illustration, J.G. Heck, 1851.

Library of Congress Cataloging-in-Publication Data
Murray, Stuart, 1948–
  The encyclopedia of war & weaponry / Stuart Murray.
      p. cm. — (Watts reference)
Summary: Chronicles the history and development of warfare and the different weapons used
throughout the centuries.
Includes bibliographical references and index.
  ISBN 0-531-12053-8 (lib. bdg.) 0-531-16382-2 (pbk.)
  1. Military art and science–Encyclopedias. 2. Military history–Encyclopedias. 3. Military
biography–Encyclopedias. 4. Military weapons–Encyclopedias. I. Title. II. Series.

U27 .M87 2002
355'.003–dc21

                                                                                    2002005302

TABLE OF CONTENTS

FRENCH COLONIAL MARINES ca. 1890 in campaign uniform; they garrisoned France's far-flung colonial empire in Africa and Asia.

INTRODUCTION

Since the dawn of history, wars have determined the course of human civilization. Simply put, war is conflict between nations or states, or between opposing political groups or religions. Civil wars and revolutions are fought between groups in the same country or under the same government.

In centuries past, many wars began over claims to territory or because a monarch tried to rule another people. In the 5th century BC, Persia's King Xerxes attempted to expand his empire by attacking the Greek city states, but he was defeated. A century later, Alexander the Great led the Greeks in the conquest of Persia.

Wars also occur because one religious group tries to convert or destroy another. During the Crusades (1099–1291), European Christians invaded the Muslim countries of the Middle East to capture holy sites, such as Jerusalem and Bethlehem. In the following centuries, the Muslim nations drove out the crusaders and invaded Christian countries.

The Muslims conquered cities and spread their culture and religion into Southern and Central Europe. By the late 1500s, the Muslim offensive had been stopped and driven back, and Christianity retook most of Europe.

Military Technology

Many wars were fought for control of trade routes and commerce. The wealthiest trading nations could afford the best weapons, warships, and military equipment—often the factors that decide who will be victorious in a war.

The longbow was once "advanced" military technology; knights in the latest steel armor won the battles of medieval times; strong stone castles, massed infantry with long pikes, and hard-charging horsemen all had their day in the history of warfare.

Beginning in the 1400s, the age of gunpowder changed everything. Firearms and cannons dominated the next four centuries of warfare. Plate armor was pierced by bullets; castles were reduced to rubble by artillery; massed infantry were wiped out by field cannons swiftly pulled into action by

SINCE THE DAWN OF HISTORY
Ancient Egyptian warriors march to battle

TRAINED FOOT SOLDIERS
Americans and British cross bayonets at Yorktown

horses; and gallant cavalry charges broke against the ranks of trained foot soldiers armed with bayonet-tipped muskets and supported by cannons.

Then, in the mid-1800s, steam power and the vast manufacturing capacity of the industrial revolution again drastically changed warfare.

The Industrialization of War

Now, battleships made of steel and driven by steam could go where they wished, without need for favorable winds. Steam-powered railroad trains could transport entire armies into battle in a matter of days, even hours. And the telegraph offered instant communication from headquarters to battlefield.

Firearms and cannons, larger and more powerful than ever, were mass-produced in great quantities by the richest nations, whose military and industrial might grew far beyond that of less-advanced peoples. Well-armed Western countries developed spheres of influence throughout the world, enlarging their empires by warring with one another and with native peoples. By the early 20th century, industry had harnessed electricity, which further advanced military technology.

In World War I (1914–18), armor-plated tanks appeared, and the rapid-firing machine gun became the dominant weapon against infantry attacks. Devastating artillery bom-bardments made troops dig deeper into trenches and bunkers to avoid barrages. The war became a stalemate marked by suicidal frontal attacks that got nowhere. The airplane also arrived in World War I, quickly developing speed, range, firepower, and bomb capacity.

As motorized vehicles came into general use, oil and gasoline were essential to modern nations. Thus, underground oil reserves around the world became one of the most important resources to fight for and control. Further, leading political systems clashed in the mid-20th century. The Fascist dictators of Germany, Japan, and Italy sought to destroy both the Communist system of the Soviet Union and the Western democracies led by the United States and Great Britain.

The stage was set for World War II (1939–45).

Modern Warfare

It was not to be static trench warfare this time. Battles were decided by maneuverability, surprise, air raids, and tremendous firepower—from land and air—aimed at the point of attack.

In World War II, each side had larger and faster tanks, divisions of quick-moving motorized infantry, the deadly submarine, swarms of fighter aircraft, heavy bombers, wireless radio communications—all dedicated to the tactics of speed. The Germans called it *blitzkrieg,* or "lightning war." Air

THE INDUSTRIALIZATION OF WAR
French heavy artillery fires during World War I

NAVAL POWER
World War II U.S. aircraft carriers in the Pacific

power brought destruction to civilians, cities, and industrial complexes far from the battlefront. Now, it was entire nations that made war, not just armies and navies.

Through the second half of the 20th century, developments in television, satellites, and other communications brought about immense improvements in military systems. As the Communist Bloc faced off with the West for another possible conflict, firepower and armament surpassed anything known in the "conventional wars" of recent generations. Militaries built war machines using aerospace technology, nuclear explosives, nuclear power, ballistic missiles, and they employed sophisticated information-gathering methods and espionage.

Computer science arrived to unite and control it all.

A standoff—or "Cold War"—came to be because both sides possessed highly advanced military technology that could destroy the world. Fear of nuclear devastation helped prevent a third world war.

Unconventional Warfare

Despite advanced military technology, the initiative in modern war often belongs to the fanatical resistance fighter with an assault rifle or a home-made bomb.

Guerrillas who are dedicated to a cause ambush soldiers, destroy equipment, and even manage to overthrow governments. Terrorists unexpectedly launch attacks, sacrificing themselves in order to blow up buildings or kill people. The terrorists' objective is to create fear, so their enemies will give up and accept their demands.

Today's military must be prepared for both conventional war and nuclear war, and also for "unconventional" war with guerrillas and terrorists. Some servicemen and women are highly trained as "special forces" combat teams, which are capable of close combat with guerrillas and terrorists on their own territory. Yet, the modern military needs more than combat personnel. Many day-to-day duties are carried out at a desk or in a maintenance shop. Most military tasks are not glamorous or exciting. They are often tedious, and many are extremely demanding.

Still, every task must be done effectively, whether the individual is a sonar operator in a submarine, an aircraft mechanic on an air base, a computer specialist stationed in a distant land, or a private guarding the entrance to a military base. As part of a complex system of organization, operations, and control, every individual's duty is essential to the efficiency and success of the modern military.

When the day comes that wars are no longer profitable, no longer a way to advance a cause or build an empire, then the military will have accomplished its most important duty of all: that is, keeping the peace, everywhere in the world. ∎

MODERN WARFARE
A missile is test-fired from a U.S. warship

UNCONVENTIONAL WARFARE
U.N. peacekeepers keep watch in the Middle East

CHRONOLOGY OF WAR

Ancient Worlds (4100BC–500BC)

ca. 4100BC	Metallurgy developed: beginning of Bronze Age
ca. 3100BC	First recorded war; Pharaoh Narmer unites upper and lower Egypt
ca. 2500BC	Bow and arrow used in warfare
ca. 3000BC	Battle-chariots developed by Sumerians
ca. 1300BC	Egyptian-Hittite War
ca. 1200BC	Trojan War
ca. 1200BC	Iron weapons introduced

Classical Worlds (500BC–476AD)

499–401BC	Persian-Greek Wars
490BC	Battle of Marathon
480BC	Battle of Salamis
480BC	Battle of Thermopylae
479BC	Battle of Plataea
458BC	First Peloponnesian War
431–404BC	Great Peloponnesian War
414–413BC	Siege of Syracuse
405BC	Battle of Aegospotami
400BC	Early use of catapults
333BC	Battle of Issus
331BC	Battle of Arbela
264–146BC	Punic War
ca. 250BC	Roman infantry organized into legions
216BC	Battle of Cannae
202BC	Battle of Zama
197BC	Battle of Cynoscephalae
52BC	Siege of Alesia
31BC	Battle of Actium
9AD	Battle of Teutoberg Forest
73AD	Siege of Masada
ca. 125AD	Hadrian's Wall built
260AD	Battle of Edessa
378AD	Battle of Adrianople
410AD	Sack of Rome by Alaric
451AD	Battle of Chalons

Middle Ages (477–1453)

503–05, 524–31	Byzantine-Persian War
700	Stirrups introduced in the West
730	Franks-Moors War
732	Battle of Tours
778	Battle of Roncesvalles
751	Battle of Talas River
800	Knorr, Viking ship, developed
850	Crossbow used in France
1066	Battle of Hastings
1099–1291	The Crusades
1161	Gunpowder used in China
1191	Battle of Arsouf
1240	Russo-Swedish War
1250	Plate armor introduced
1250	Battle of Mansura
1296–1314	Wars for Scottish Independence
ca. 1300	English long bow perfected
1314	Battle of Bannockburn
1315	Battle of Mortgarten
ca. 1320	Gunpowder artillery introduced in Europe
1337–1453	Hundred Years War
1346	Battle of Crécy
1346–47	Siege of Calais
ca. 1350	Ship-borne artillery introduced in Europe

1356	Battle of Poitiers
1368	Yuan-Ming Dynasty War
1372	Battle of Rochelle
ca. 1372	Galleys, warships propelled with sail and oars common in Mediterranean
1396	Battle of Nicopolis
1415	Battle of Agincourt
1428–1429	Siege of Orleans
ca. 1450	Matchlock firearms introduced
1453	Siege of Constantinople by Turks

Renaissance and Reformation (1453–1648)

1455–1485	Wars of the Roses
1463	Turco-Venetian War
1485	Battle of Bosworth Field
ca. 1490	Rifled gun barrel invented
1495	Battle of Fornovo
ca. 1500	Artillery on wheeled carriages becomes common
1502–1515	Franco-Spanish Wars
1515	Battle of Marignano
1512–1522	Russo-Polish War
1521	Battle of Tenochititlán
1525	Great Mortar of Moscow built
1531–1537	Spanish conquest of Peru
1535	Siege of Tunis
1535–1538	Spanish-Moorish War
1536–1537	Battles of Cuzco
1562–1598	French Religious Wars
1568–1648	Eight Years' War
1571	Battle of Lepanto
1574	Siege of Leyden
1587–1603	Anglo-Spanish War
1588	Spanish Armada defeated
1600–1603	Japanese Civil War
1600	Battle of Sekigahara
1618–1648	Thirty Years War
ca. 1600	Infantry carry either matchlock muskets or pikes
1627–28	Siege of La Rochelle
1631	Battle of Breitenfeld I
1631	Battle of Leipzig

1642–48	Civil War in England
1642	Battle of Edgehill
1643	Battle of Rocroi
1644	Battle of Marston Moor
1645	Battle of Naseby

Age of Kings (1649–1789)

1652–74	Anglo-Dutch Wars
1658	Battle of the Dunes
1675	King Philip's War
1675	Battle of Fehrbellin
1685	Turkish Siege of Vienna
1690	Battle of the Boyne
1692	Battle of La Hogue
ca. 1700	Flintlock muskets with bayonets become standard infantry weapon
1700–1721	Great Northern War
1700	Battle of Narva
1701–1713	War of the Spanish Succession
1702	Queen Anne's War
1704	Battle of Blenheim
1706	Battle of Ramillies
1708	Siege of Lille
1709	Battle of Poltava
1739–1741	War of Jenkin's Ear
1740–1748	War of the Austrian Succession
1743	Battle of Dettingen
1744–1748	King George's War
1745	Siege of Louisburg
1745	Battle of Fontenoy
1745	Battle of Hohenfriedburg
1746	Battle of Culloden
ca. 1750	Horse artillery introduced into Prussian army
1755–1763	French and Indian War
1756–1763	Seven Years War
1757	Battle of Rossbach
1757	Battle of Leuthen
1757	Battle of Plassey
1758	Battle of Ticonderoga
1759	Battle of Quebec
1775–1783	American Revolution

1775	Battles of Lexington and Concord
1775	Battle of Breed's (Bunker) Hill
1776	Battle of Trenton
1776	First submarine used in warfare
1776	Battle of Long Island
1777	Battles of Saratoga
1778	Battle of Ushant
1779–83	Siege of Gibraltar
1781	Battle of the Cowpens
1781	Siege of Yorktown

Age of Revolution (1790–1815)

1792–1802	French Revolutionary Wars
1792	Battle of Valmy
1797	Battle of Cape St. Vincent
1798	Battle of the Nile
1800	Battle of Marengo
1803	Battle of Assaye
1804–1815	Napoleonic Wars
1805	Battle of Trafalgar
1805	Battle of Austerlitz
1806	Battles of Jena and Auerstadt
1807	First steamboat voyage
1807	Battle of Eylau
1807–1814	Peninsular War
1811–1814	War for Venezuelan Independence
1812–1814	War of 1812
1812	Battle of Thames River (Canada)
1812	Napoleon's invasion of Russia
1812	Battle of Borodino (Moscow)
1812	Battle of the Berezina
1813	Battle of Dresden
1813	Battle of Lake Erie
1813	Battle of Leipzig
1814	Battle of Lundy's Lane
1815	Battle of New Orleans
1815	Battle of Waterloo

Age of Nationalism (1816–1871)

1821–1829	Greek War of Independence
1821	Battle of Carabobo
1822–1824	Algerian Wars
1827	Battle of Navarino
1830–1843	Seminole Wars
1835–36	War of Texan Independence
1836	Siege of the Alamo
1836	Battle of San Jacinto
1837–42	Opium War
ca. 1842	Anglo-Afghan Wars
1845	Battle of Ferozshah
1846–1848	Mexican War
1846	Battle of Buena Vista
1847	Battles for Mexico City
ca. 1849	Prussian "needle gun" introduced
ca. 1850	Percussion rifle muskets become standard infantry weapon
1854–1856	Crimean War
1854	Battle of Balaklava
1854	Battle of Inkerman
1854–55	Siege of Sevastopol
1857	Indian Mutiny
1857	First "ironclad" warship, *Gloiré*, launched by France
1859	Battle of Solferino
1860–66	Italian War of Independence
1861–1865	U.S. Civil War
1861, 1862	Battles of Bull Run
1862	Battle of Shiloh
1862	Battle of Hampton Roads, first clash of ironclad warships
1862	Observation balloons used by Union Army
1862	Seven Day's Battles
1862	Battle of Antietam
1862	Battle of Fredericksburg
1862	Gatling repeat-fire gun invented
1863	Seven-shot Spencer repeating rifle introduced
1863	Battle of Chancellorsville
1863	Battle of Gettysburg
ca. 1863	Breech-loading artillery used in combat
1863	Siege of Vicksburg
1863	Battle of Puebla

1863	Battle of Chickamaugua
1864	Battles of Atlanta
1864–1865	Siege of Petersburg
1864	U.S. Army uses Parrott gun
1864–1865	"Dictator," 13-inch mortar used by Union forces at Petersburg
1864–1870	War of the Triple Alliance
1866	Seven Week's War
1866	Battle of Köninggratz
1868	Battle of the Washita
1868–1890	Indian Wars in the West
1870–1871	Franco-Prussian War
1870	Battle and siege of Sedan
1870–1871	Siege of Paris

Age of Colonialism (1872–1913)

1876	Battle of the Little Bighorn
1877	Battle of Plevna
1879	Zulu War
1879	Battle of Isandhlwana
1879–1883	War of the Pacific (South America)
ca. 1880	Single-shot breechloading rifles become standard infantry weapon
1880–1902	Boer Wars
1884–1885	Siege of Khartoum
1884	Maxim machine gun developed in England
1887	First automobile introduced
1894–1895	Sino-Japanese War
1896	British Sudanese campaigns
1896	Battle of Omdurman
1898	Spanish-American War
1898	Battle of San Juan Hill
1898	Battle of Manila Bay
ca. 1900	Bolt-action, magazine-fed rifles become standard infantry weapon
ca. 1900	First successful naval submarines
1900	Chinese Boxer Rebellion
1900	Battle of Bloemfontein
1903	First airplane flight
1904–05	Russo-Japanese War
1904–05	Siege of Port Arthur
1905	Battle of Tsushima Strait
1906	First modern battleship launched HMS *Dreadnought*
1912–1913	Balkan Wars

The World Wars (1914–1945)

1914–18	World War I
1914	French 75mm gun is basic artillery weapon
1914, 1918	Battles of the Marne
1914	Battle of Tannenberg
1914, '15, '17	Battles of Ypres
1915	German submarines sink merchant ships without warning
1915	Germans use chlorine poison gas
1915	Germans introduce Fokker LVG-CVI fighter plane
1915	Gallipoli campaign
1916	Battle of Jutland
1916	Battle of Verdun
1916	Battle of the Somme
1916	First use of tank in battle at Cambrai
1917	U.S. enters World War I
1917	Battle of Caporetto
1917–22	Russian Civil War
ca. 1917	First use of aircraft for strategic bombing
1918	German offensives on the Western Front
1918	Battle of St. Mihiel
1927	Aircraft carriers added to U.S. Navy
1935–1936	Ethiopian-Italian War
1935	Radar used to detect aircraft
1936–1939	Spanish Civil War
ca. 1937	German BF-109 fighter introduced
ca. 1938	British Spitfire introduced
ca. 1939	B-17 bomber introduced
1939	First experimental helicopter flights
1939–1940	Russo-Finnish War
1939–1945	World War II
1940	Battle of France
1940	Dunkirk Retreat

1940	Battle of Britain
1940	Garand M-1 semi-automatic rifle introduced
1940	First use of paratroopers in combat
1941–1943	Battle of the Atlantic
1941–42	Battles of Tobruk
1941	German invasion of Soviet Union, operation "Barbarossa"
1941–1944	Siege of Leningrad
1941	Japanese attack on Pearl Harbor
1941	M-38 utility vehicle, the "Jeep," introduced
1942	Battle of Bataan and subsequent Death March of U.S. prisoners
1942	General Doolittle's air raid on Tokyo
1942	Battle of El Alamein
1942	Battle of Midway
1942	Battle of Kasserine Pass
1942	Sherman tank in service with U.S. and British armies
1942–1943	Battle of Guadalcanal
1942	U.S. Women's Army Corps (WAC) created
1942–43	Battle of Stalingrad
1943	Battle of Kursk
1943	MP-43 Sturmgewehr assault rifle introduced by Germany
1943	Allies invade Italy
1944	P-51 judged best fighter plane
1944–45	Germany launches V-2 guided missiles at Britain
1944	D-Day Invasion of France
1944	Battle of Leyte Gulf
1944	Battle of Arnhem
1944	Battle of the Bulge
1944	First combat use of jet aircraft (by Germany)
1945	Battle of Iwo Jima
1945	Battle of Okinawa
1945	Battle of Berlin
1945	Atomic bombs are dropped on Hiroshima and Nagasaki

The Cold War World (1946–1989)

1945–1949	Chinese Civil War
1946–1949	Greek Civil War
1947–54	Indochina War
1950–53	Korean War
1950	Inchon Landing
1952	Hydrogen bomb tested
1954–1962	Algerian war for independence
1953–54	Siege of Dien Bien Phu
1954	First nuclear powered submarine launched
1957	USSR launches first ICBM (Intercontinental Ballistic Missile)
1957	U.S.S.R. launches Sputnik satellite
1948,1956, 1967,1973	Arab-Israeli Wars
1960	Trident BGM-109 sea-launched Tomahawk cruise missile introduced
1960s	M-16-A1 5.6mm rifle adopted by U.S.
1962–1975	Vietnam War
1967–1970	Nigerian Civil War
1967	Six Day's War
1968	Siege of Khe Sanh
1968	Tet Offensive
1972	First use of laser-guided "smart" bombs
1973	Yom Kippur War
1975	U.S. leaves Vietnam
1979–1989	Russian-Afghan War
1980s	M1 Abrams heavy tank introduced
1982	Falklands War
1980–88	Iran-Iraq War
1989	Berlin Wall demolished

Today's World (1990–)

1990–1991	Gulf War
1990s	B-2 Stealth bomber introduced
1991	First combat use of cruise missiles
1991–93	U.S. troops in Somalia
1991–2000	Balkan Wars of Independence
2001	War on Terrorism

EUROPE, THE MEDITERRANEAN, NORTH AFRICA AND THE MIDDLE EAST

FINLAND

NORWAY

SWEDEN

• Stockholm

ESTONIA

SCOTLAND

■ Culloden 1745

North Sea

LATVIA

Copenhagen •

IRELAND

DENMARK

Baltic Sea

LITHUANIA

■ Marston Moor 1644

ENGLAND

Amsterdam •

Prussia

POLAND

ATLANTIC OCEAN

• London

THE NETHERLANDS

• Berlin

• Warsaw

Hastings 1066 ■

BELGIUM

English Channel

■ Waterloo 1815

GERMANY

Normandy Invasion (D-Day) 1944 ■

Crécy 1346 ■ Agincourt 1415

Saxony

Somme 1916 ■

■ Battle of the Bulge 1944

E   U   R   O   P   E

Paris •

Austerlitz 1805 ■

Tours 732 ■ • Orléans

Verdun 1916 ■

Blenheim 1704 ■

Bohemia

Bay of Biscay

Poitiers 1356 ■

Bavaria

Vienna • ■ Wagram 1809

FRANCE

SWITZERLAND

AUSTRIA

(GAUL)

Alps Mts.

HUNGARY

Pyrenees Mts.

• Venice

ROMANIA

Croatia

Adriatic Sea

YUGOSLAVIA

ITALY

Sarajevo •

Serbia

• Lisbon

• Madrid

Corsica

Bosnia

PORTUGAL

SPAIN

• Rome

Macedonia

■ Cannae 216BC

ALBANIA

Sardinia

Trafalgar 1805 ■

Thermopylae 480BC ■

• Gibraltar

GREECE

Athens •

Sicily

Sparta

Carthage

MOROCCO

ALGERIA

Mediterranean Sea

Atlas Mts.

TUNISIA

A   F   R   I   C   A

The maps on page 14–17 show countries, regions, and major geographical features. Red squares indicate battle sites. Historic place names are shown in a gray tint.

St. Petersburg
(Leningrad)

Borodino 1812 ■   • Moscow

RUSSIA
(SOVIET UNION)

Aral Sea

UKRAINE

■ Poltava 1709

Stalingrad 1942–43

A   S   I   A

Caspian Sea

Crimea

Chechnya

Caucasus Mts.

• Sevastopol

Black Sea

BULGARIA

AFGHANISTAN

Istanbul
(Constantinople)

IRAN
(PERSIA)

TURKEY

ASSYRIA

■ Issus 333BC

Adriatic
Sea

SYRIA

Baghdad •

Crete

Cyprus

■ Kadesh 1296BC

IRAQ
(MESOPOTAMIA)

KUWAIT

ISRAEL
Jerusalem • JORDAN
Alexandria •
Palestine

A   S   I   A

Persian Gulf

■ El Alamein 1942
Cairo •   Sinai

SAUDI
ARABIA

EGYPT

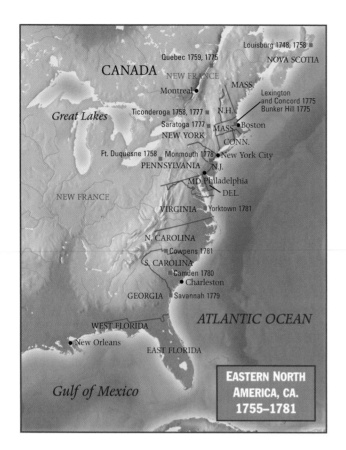

Louisburg 1748, 1758
NOVA SCOTIA
Quebec 1759, 1775
CANADA
NEW FRANCE
Montreal
MASS.
Great Lakes
Ticonderoga 1758, 1777
N.H.
Lexington and Concord 1775
Bunker Hill 1775
Saratoga 1777
MASS. Boston
NEW YORK
CONN.
Ft. Duquesne 1758
Monmouth 1778
New York City
PENNSYLVANIA
N.J.
MD Philadelphia
NEW FRANCE
DEL.
VIRGINIA
Yorktown 1781
N. CAROLINA
Cowpens 1781
S. CAROLINA
Camden 1780
Charleston
GEORGIA
Savannah 1779
WEST FLORIDA
New Orleans
EAST FLORIDA
ATLANTIC OCEAN
Gulf of Mexico

EASTERN NORTH AMERICA, CA. 1755–1781

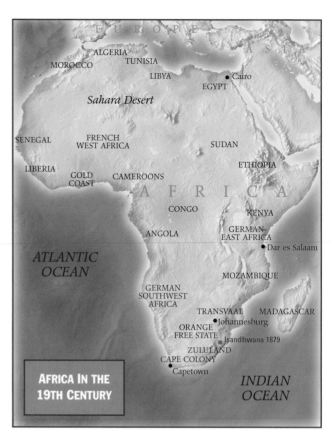

EUROPE
ASIA
ALGERIA
TUNISIA
MOROCCO
LIBYA
EGYPT
Cairo
Sahara Desert
SENEGAL
FRENCH WEST AFRICA
SUDAN
LIBERIA
GOLD COAST
CAMEROONS
ETHIOPIA
A F R I C A
CONGO
KENYA
ATLANTIC OCEAN
ANGOLA
GERMAN EAST AFRICA
Dar es Salaam
MOZAMBIQUE
GERMAN SOUTHWEST AFRICA
TRANSVAAL
MADAGASCAR
Johannesburg
ORANGE FREE STATE
Isandlhwana 1879
ZULULAND
CAPE COLONY
Capetown
INDIAN OCEAN

AFRICA IN THE 19TH CENTURY

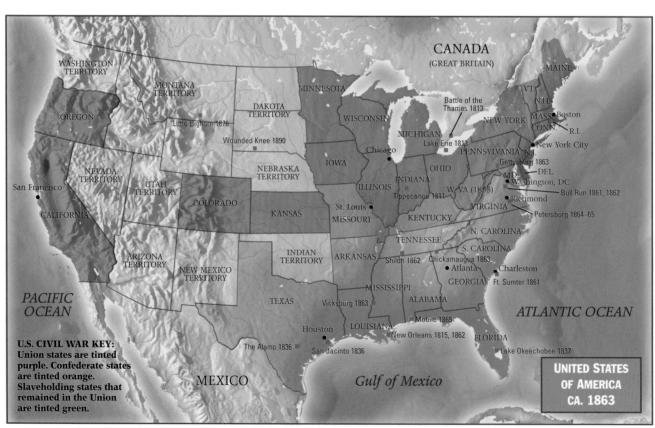

CANADA
(GREAT BRITAIN)
WASHINGTON TERRITORY
MAINE
MONTANA TERRITORY
MINNESOTA
VT.
N.H.
DAKOTA TERRITORY
WISCONSIN
Battle of the Thames 1813
NEW YORK
MASS. Boston
OREGON
CONN.
R.I.
Little Bighorn 1876
MICHIGAN
Lake Erie 1813
PENNSYLVANIA
N.J.
New York City
Wounded Knee 1890
Chicago
Gettysburg 1863
NEVADA TERRITORY
NEBRASKA TERRITORY
IOWA
OHIO
MD DEL.
Washington, DC
UTAH TERRITORY
INDIANA
W. VA (1865)
Bull Run 1861, 1862
San Francisco
ILLINOIS
Tippecanoe 1811
Richmond
COLORADO
St. Louis
VIRGINIA
Petersburg 1864–65
CALIFORNIA
KANSAS
MISSOURI
KENTUCKY
N. CAROLINA
ARIZONA TERRITORY
INDIAN TERRITORY
ARKANSAS
TENNESSEE
S. CAROLINA
Chickamauga 1863
NEW MEXICO TERRITORY
Shiloh 1862
Atlanta
Charleston
GEORGIA
Ft. Sumter 1861
MISSISSIPPI
ALABAMA
PACIFIC OCEAN
TEXAS
Vicksburg 1863
Mobile 1865
ATLANTIC OCEAN
Houston
LOUISIANA
New Orleans 1815, 1862
FLORIDA
The Alamo 1836
San Jacinto 1836
Lake Okeechobee 1837
MEXICO
Gulf of Mexico

U.S. CIVIL WAR KEY:
Union states are tinted purple. Confederate states are tinted orange. Slaveholding states that remained in the Union are tinted green.

UNITED STATES OF AMERICA CA. 1863

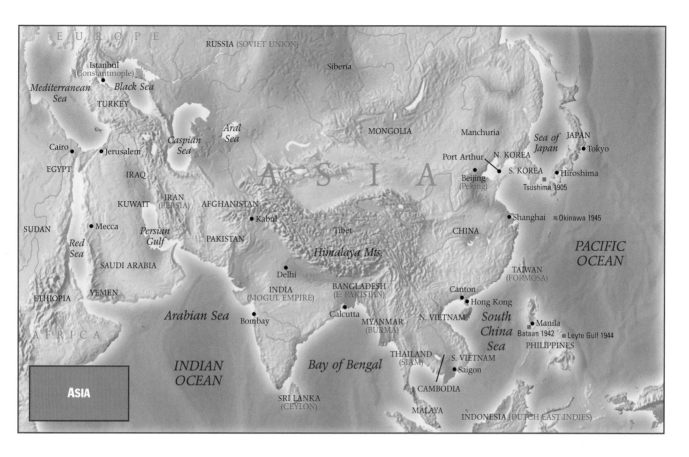

E U R O P E

RUSSIA (SOVIET UNION)

Siberia

Istanbul
(Constantinople)

*Mediterranean
Sea*
Black Sea

TURKEY

*Caspian
Sea*

*Aral
Sea*

MONGOLIA

Manchuria

*Sea of
Japan*

JAPAN

• Tokyo

Port Arthur
• N. KOREA
• S. KOREA
• Hiroshima

A   S   I   A

Beijing
(Peking)

Tsushima 1905

Cairo
• Jerusalem

EGYPT

IRAQ

IRAN
(PERSIA)

AFGHANISTAN

KUWAIT

• Kabul

• Shanghai ■ Okinawa 1945

CHINA

*PACIFIC
OCEAN*

SUDAN

• Mecca

*Persian
Gulf*

PAKISTAN

Tibet

TAIWAN
(FORMOSA)

*Red
Sea*

SAUDI ARABIA

Himalaya Mts.

• Delhi

Canton •
• Hong Kong

ETHIOPIA

YEMEN

A F R I C A

Arabian Sea

INDIA
(MOGUL EMPIRE)

BANGLADESH
(E. PAKISTAN)

Calcutta
•

Bombay •

MYANMAR
(BURMA)

N. VIETNAM

*South
China
Sea*

■ • Manila
Bataan 1942 ■ Leyte Gulf 1944

PHILIPPINES

*INDIAN
OCEAN*

Bay of Bengal

THAILAND
(SIAM)

S. VIETNAM
• Saigon

CAMBODIA

ASIA

SRI LANKA
(CEYLON)

MALAYA

INDONESIA (DUTCH EAST INDIES)

Cartagena •

VENEZUELA

Bogotá
•
COLOMBIA
(NEW GRANADA)

• Cayenne

GUIANA

ECUADOR

S O U T H   A M E R I C A

PERU

• Lima

BRAZIL
(EMPIRE OF BRAZIL)

BOLIVIA

INCA EMPIRE
• La Paz

PARAGUAY

• Rio de Janiero

CHILE

Santiago •

URUGUAY

• Montevideo
Buenos Aires

Patagonia

ARGENTINA

*ATLANTIC
OCEAN*

*PACIFIC
OCEAN*

**SOUTH
AMERICA**

Falkland Islands
(Islas Malvinas)

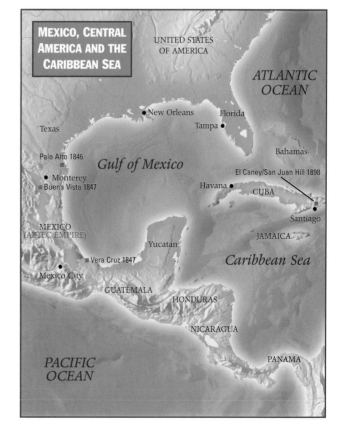

**MEXICO, CENTRAL
AMERICA AND THE
CARIBBEAN SEA**

UNITED STATES
OF AMERICA

*ATLANTIC
OCEAN*

• New Orleans
Florida

Texas

Tampa
•

Bahamas

Palo Alto 1846

Gulf of Mexico

El Caney/San Juan Hill 1898

• Monterey
■ Buena Vista 1847

Havana •

CUBA

■
Santiago

MEXICO
(AZTEC EMPIRE)

Yucatan

JAMAICA

■ Vera Cruz 1847

Caribbean Sea

• Mexico City

GUATEMALA

HONDURAS

*PACIFIC
OCEAN*

NICARAGUA

PANAMA

Airborne Troops

After **World War I** (1914–18), Russia and Germany developed the first paratroopers—soldiers who parachute into combat from airplanes. Britain established its paratrooper regiments in 1940, after the start of **World War II** (1939–45), and the first United States paratrooper units appeared in 1941.

Paratroopers, also termed airborne troops, are elite soldiers whose rigorous training prepares them for the dangers of the jump itself, as well as for operations in enemy-held territory. Paratroopers are used to capture important objectives, such as bridges and communications centers, and to hold them until ground troops arrive.

Early Russian paratroopers had to crawl along the wing of a plane, holding on to handles, then slide off the wing and open their chutes. Later, paratroopers leaped from a door in the side of the airplane, which was far safer. The first notable paratroop assault occurred in World War II, during the Nazi invasion of the Netherlands in 1940, when German parachute troops dropped behind Dutch lines. The first great airborne assault was part of the May 1941 German capture of the island of Crete in the Mediterranean. In 1944, Allied paratroopers were crucial to the success of the Normandy invasion.

Some modern airborne units, often known as "air cavalry," are equipped with fast, heavily armed **helicopters** that quickly discharge or pick up troops in a battle zone while being protected by powerful gunship helicopters accompanying the mission. ■

Aircraft Carriers

Aircraft carriers are "airfields at sea" with special equipment for warplanes to take off and land, such as catapults on the flight deck that help launch the plane, and wires across the deck to bring a landing plane to a stop.

In 1910, the American navy began experimenting with takeoffs and landings from flight decks built on ships. Late in **World War I** (1914–18), the British Navy converted a merchant vessel into the first true aircraft carrier. The U.S. and Japanese navies soon followed, building new vessels designed as aircraft carriers. The first of these was Japan's *Hosyo,* launched in 1922.

The first combat use of aircraft carriers was the Japanese air attack on the American naval base at Pearl Harbor, Hawaii, on December 7, 1941. The American and British navies raced to construct more carriers, including light carriers for anti-submarine

FLOATING AIRFIELDS
American aircraft carriers loaded with airplanes plow through the seas on a Korean War mission. The carriers are accompanied by warships that guard against submarine attacks. The wings of the aircraft on the carriers' decks are folded to take up less room.

AIRCRAFT

Air power includes strategic bombing–high-level bombing of targets such as military bases and manufacturing centers–and tactical strikes–close air support of troops on the ground, and attacks on enemy shipping, equipment, and positions. Combat aircraft also engage each other to battle for control of the skies.

Military flights began in the mid-19th century, with observation balloons carrying spotters high above the armies to see beyond the enemy's front lines. In **World War I** (1914–18), recently invented fixed-wing aircraft were used for observation at first, but they quickly developed into deadly weapons, increasing their speed, firepower, and bomb capacity. By **World War II** (1939–45), airpower was key to every military force, and aircraft design continued to improve.

In the late 1940s, jet propulsion engines made fighters supersonic, able to fly faster than the speed of sound. By the 1960s, British-made **Harrier Jets** could take off and land vertically, without the need for runways. Long-range bombers flew missions of more than 5,000 miles, and unmanned "spy planes" soared high above the range of anti-aircraft fire to observe and photograph enemy positions.

One of the first military aircraft, this Union observation balloon of the Civil War is being filled with hydrogen gas; it will soon be sent aloft carrying men with telescopes.

A German fighter begins to nose dive and crash after being strafed by the machine guns of a French Spad during World War I action.

American B-17 "Flying Fortress" long-range bombers roar above Nazi Germany in World War II, as Allied P-38 fighter planes patrol nearby, keeping enemy fighters away from the bombers.

This U.S. Air Force F-111 fighter bomber returns to base after a strike on Iraqi ground forces in Saudi Arabia in 1991.

A

operations which were essential to the Allied triumph over the Axis powers in **World War II** (1939–45).

After the war, carriers became ever larger. In the 1970s, light carriers also served as bases for **helicopter** fleets and for launching amphibious assaults. In the 1990s, aircraft carriers supported United Nations forces in the **Persian Gulf War,** and in 2001 were key bases for American and British operations in the Afghanistan conflict. ■

Alexander III, the Great (356–323BC)

One of history's most famous military leaders was Alexander, King of Macedonia, who led the Greeks in the conquest of the Persian empire between 334–330BC. Alexander also conquered Egypt and founded the city of Alexandria at the mouth of the Nile. Pushing eastward, he entered India, where his advance was stopped in 326BC.

Though usually outnumbered in battle, Alexander won victories that stand with the greatest military achievements of all time. Alexander's Macedonian spearmen, equipped with 16-foot pikes, fought in tight, disciplined squares known as **phalanxes,** which drove powerfully through enemy ranks. It was Alexander's cavalry,

ALEXANDER DEFEATS DARIUS
This Roman mosaic portrays the 333BC victory of Alexander over Persian emperor Darius III at the Battle of Issus in Syria. Darius lost several conflicts, and finally his empire, to Alexander, pictured at left.

however, that often dealt the decisive blow in a battle.

Alexander died of fever in 323BC, at the age of 33. He brought Greek (Hellenic) culture to a vast region, stretching from Europe to India and Egypt. The peoples of this empire created centers of civilization based on Hellenic culture, and the merchant's road between Europe and Asia was opened thanks to the conquests of Alexander the Great. ■

Alexander the Great's Asiatic Wars

Conflict between Greeks and Persians had continued for centuries when Alexander III became king of Macedonia in 336BC. Ruled by King Darius III, the Persian empire stretched from Turkey and Iran southward through the western Mediterranean countries to Egypt.

Alexander defeated Darius's army in 333BC, when 30,000 Greeks overcame 100,000 Persians at Issus. Alexander captured Egypt, a Persian dominion, and in 331BC again defeated Darius, this time with only 47,000 men against 200,000.

From here, Alexander moved eastward, winning victories, enlisting allies, establishing governments, and finally reaching India in 327BC. Accompanying Alexander's army were scientists, historians, **engineers,** and surveyors. He brought Greek culture to the peoples he conquered, and established cities that became strongholds for his empire as well as colonies of Greek democratic rule.

Alexander invaded India, but his Macedonian troops, sick of campaigning, would go no further and compelled him to turn back. Three years later he died of fever in Babylon. ■

American Revolutionary War

Also known as the American War of Independence, the Revolutionary War was a conflict between Great Britain and 13 North American colonies. The war became

global, with Britain opposed by France, Spain, and the Dutch Republic, and it ended in American independence.

The main cause was Britain's attempt to limit American liberties, control colonial growth and development, and levy taxes and duties without the consent of colonial governing bodies. King George III and the dominant Tory party tried to govern the American colonies from London, but armed rebellion broke out in April 1775. Under the leadership of Commander-in-chief **George Washington,** the revolutionary army developed into hard-hitting troops able to stand up to professional British regulars.

Key American victories included Washington's siege of Boston in 1775–76, and his surprise counterattacks at Trenton and Princeton, New Jersey, in the winter of 1776–77. France allied itself with the rebellious colonies in 1778 and went to war against Britain. In October 1781, the decisive victory of the war took place when Washington and his French allies trapped and defeated General Charles Cornwallis's army at Yorktown, Virginia. ■

Anglo-Afghan Wars

The Central Asian country of Afghanistan is a crossroads for trade and warfare, and was a prize sought by both Britain and Russia in the 19th century.

The British attempted to control Afghanistan and stop the southward expansion of Russia. British imperial troops invaded Afghanistan in 1839 in an alliance with the former king, who had been deposed. The British army and the Afghan king could not pacify the country, however, and the following year 4,500 imperial soldiers occupying Kabul were massacred. British forces recaptured Kabul, but the soldiers soon withdrew from Afghanistan to avoid continued warfare.

The Second Anglo-Afghan War began in 1878, when the Afghan government befriended the Russians and became hostile to the British. The British won victories in the first phase of this war, occupying Kabul. Fighting continued until 1881, when an Afghan leader who was a British ally finally took control of the country. In

THE GENERAL'S LIFE GUARD

George Washington's bodyguard during the Revolutionary War was made up of picked men and known as the "Life Guard." Most were officers, many of them from Washington's home state of Virginia. The Life Guards camped at Washington's headquarters, often in the yard or gardens of private homes the general chose for his quarters. They were outstanding soldiers, chosen for their loyalty to Washington. The Life Guard had to be alert because more than once, the British plotted to assassinate Washington.

A COSTLY REDCOAT VICTORY Maryland soldiers prepare for an assault by the Redcoat army of General Charles Cornwallis at Guilford Courthouse, North Carolina, in 1781. Cornwallis forced the withdrawal of the Americans—commanded by General Nathanael Greene, shown on horseback—but more than 530 British were killed or wounded, while the Americans suffered 260 casualties.

A

ARMOR

Suit of armor from the Castle of Churburg, Southern Tyrol, Italy, ca. 1390. The suit includes a bascinet-style helmet. In the right hand is a pole arm known as a bardiche.

Armor is body-covering that protects a combatant in battle. The first armor was made of leather, horn, bone, iron, and thick fabric, and some ancient Chinese wore coats of rhinoceros skin. **Mail** shirts, sometimes called "chain mail," were made of small, interwoven iron loops. Flexible and fairly lightweight, mail was used for centuries by soldiers from Europe to East Asia.

In the 13th century, **plate armor** appeared in response to improvements in edged weapons and as a way to deflect increasingly powerful missiles, such as the crossbow bolt. Firearms forced armorers to further thicken plates during the 16th and 17th centuries, but the increased weight made armor too heavy for combat. As warfare became dominated by firearms in the 17th century, soldiers needed mobility, so most armor was abandoned. By the 18th century, little armor was in use militarily other than the cavalryman's helmet and the cuirass for his chest and back.

In **World War I** (1914–18), steel helmets were issued to infantry as protection from overhead shell bursts. After **World War II** (1939–45), bulletproof "flak jackets" were introduced as armor to protect the soldier's upper body.

Roman imperial legionary of the 1st century AD. He wears the classic Imperial Gallic helmet and complex shoulder and torso armor known as a *lorica segmentata*. The shield or *scutum*, spear or *pilum*, and sword or *gladius* complete his armament.

Wearing a protective flak jacket, an Egyptian marine storms a beach during amphibious-assault training in 2001.

French carabiniers ca.1870 with helmets and torso protection. The mounted trooper wears a metal *cuirass*; the drummer's coat has musician's cloth lace.

1893, Afghanistan's boundaries were drawn up by Britain and Russia.

In 1919, an uprising against outside influence again brought in British imperial troops. A month-long struggle ended with the Afghans given the right to conduct their own foreign affairs. Afghanistan soon signed a friendship pact with the new Soviet Union, becoming the first nation to recognize the communist government. ∎

Anglo-Dutch Wars

These were four conflicts between England and the Dutch Republic (United Provinces of The Netherlands) in the 17th and 18th centuries. Rivalry for control of international trade was the main reason for these wars.

The first Anglo-Dutch War (1652–54) resulted from the English attempt to bar the Dutch from independent trading with British colonies. Both sides suffered heavy losses and the war ended by treaty. The rivalry led to a second Anglo-Dutch War (1665–67), with the Dutch republic winning most of the battles. In 1667, the Dutch fleet daringly entered the River Thames and destroyed the English fleet, forcing the English to agree to peace terms.

The third Anglo-Dutch War (1672–74) was part of a broader European conflict. Several times, the Dutch defeated English fleets, thus preventing an invasion and ultimately bringing about a treaty.

The fourth Anglo-Dutch War (1780–84) was the result of Dutch support for the American Revolution. England made peace with her former colonies and also with her adversaries Holland, France, and Spain. ∎

Anti-aircraft Gun

The first artillery defenses against attack from the air were developed during **World War I** (1914–18). Field guns were converted into anti-aircraft weapons by changing their mountings to permit them to fire straight up. Next, artillery was developed to fire exploding shells, "flak," which were timed to burst near enemy aircraft.

In **World War II** (1939–45), rapid-firing anti-aircraft artillery termed "ack-ack" or "pom-pom" guns were integrated with range-finders, proximity fuses (designed to explode near the target), and searchlights. In this time, the Swedish-made Bofors anti-aircraft gun was capable of firing projectiles as high as two miles.

Later, warplanes became subject to deadly fire from radar-guided weapons that fired 45 rounds a minute and reached a height of 50,000 feet. Even more deadly is the surface-to-air missile (SAM). The surface-to-air missile is guided by radio signals and is "heat-seeking"— meaning it homes in on the target aircraft's jet exhaust. Powerful shoulder-held anti-aircraft weapons like the American "Stinger" and the British "Blowpipe," enable an average infantry-man to shoot down low-flying aircraft and **helicopters**. ∎

READY FOR AIR ATTACK The crew of a 90mm anti-aircraft artillery emplacement on the island of Okinawa prepares for action during World War II.

STINGER MISSILE American Marines launch a shoulder-fired Stinger anti-aircraft missile at a target during a live-fire exercise in California; these weapons are deadly to low-flying aircraft, especially helicopters, which hover close to the ground. Soldiers can lie in wait under cover until the enemy aircraft comes within range and fire the Stinger, which is comparable to the British Blowpipe shoulder-fired missile. During Russia's Afghanistan campaigns in in the mid-1990s, Afghan rebels using American-supplied Stingers took a heavy toll of Soviet helicopters.

A

French bombards fire stones to break open a Muslim city's walls during an assault in the 15th century.

An Armstrong Gun in Confederate-held Fort Fisher, above, defends Wilmington, North Carolina, against an 1865 Civil War attack by Union land and naval forces.

A 155mm artillery shell hurtles out of the barrel of a U.S. Marine howitzer during a live-fire exercise in the Middle East in 2000.

ARTILLERY

Artillery first appeared in medieval times, as crude guns fired spears and stones and, later, iron balls. Early in the 15th century, cannons were used mainly for **siege warfare**. Large guns known as bombards were capable of firing up to a mile. In the 16th century, improved gun design and the addition of wheels brought artillery onto the open battlefield alongside the troops.

The science of gunnery—the aiming and operation of guns—came into being in this time, pioneered in Italy. By the 17th century, gunnery science and improved gun design brought artillery to the forefront of military operations. Naval artillery became essential to merchant vessel and warship alike. (Guns based on land are called artillery, while those aboard ship are naval guns.)

The 18th and 19th centuries saw dramatic progress in the mobility, range, and accuracy of artillery pieces, and in the projectiles they used. Heavy cannons and field guns dominated early 20th-century warfare, but in modern wars, rockets and missiles and bombing from warplanes have assumed much of the fire-support role that once belonged only to cannons.

A Continental Artillery gun crew loads its field cannon for action in the Revolutionary War.

Arab-Israeli Wars

This series of conflicts resulted from Arab opposition to the creation of a Jewish state in Palestine, and involved four wars in 1948, 1956, 1967, and 1973.

Britain governed Palestine by United Nations mandate after **World War II** (1939–45), but faced conflict between Jews seeking to create a state and Arabs who were being displaced by Jewish settlers. After a period of Zionist-led terrorism that included the assassination of the United Nations commissioner, the British departed Palestine in May 1948.

The new State of Israel was immediately attacked by surrounding Arab countries in a war that ended by mid-1949 with an Israeli victory. More than 700,000 Arabs left the former Palestine and were settled in refugee camps in the Egyptian Gaza strip, Lebanon, Jordan, Syria, and Iraq. No Arab state recognized Israel, and Arab hostility remained.

In 1956, the Israeli army joined a French and British attack on Egypt in a campaign sparked by disputes over control of the strategic Suez Canal. Egypt was defeated in a few weeks. Israel took control of the Gaza Strip and the Sinai Desert, but eventually withdrew from the Sinai.

In 1967, 250,000 Egyptian troops moved toward their border with Israel. That June, Israel launched a preemptive air strike that destroyed most of the Egyptian, Syrian, Jordanian, and Iraqi air forces on the ground. Simultaneously, the Israeli army routed the Egyptian army in the Sinai Desert and Gaza and also attacked Syrian forces, driving them from the fortified Golan Heights. From Jordan, Israel took the West Bank of the Jordan River and assumed full control of Jerusalem. The Sinai Peninsula up to the Suez Canal was taken from Egypt. The conflict is known as the "Six-day War."

With the United States as Israel's main supporter, and the U.S.S.R. backing the Arab countries, hostility persisted. In October 1973, the Fourth Arab-Israeli War began, as Egyptian and Syrian forces attacked Israel during the Jewish holy days, in what became known as the "Yom Kippur War." Dominating the air, Israeli forces repulsed these offensives and went on the counterattack, threatening to take the Syrian capital of Damascus and crossing the Suez Canal. The fighting ended late in the month with a cease-fire administered by the United Nations.

Israel reached peace terms with Egypt in 1979 and eventually withdrew from the Sinai, but the Middle East remained heavily armed and in a constant state of tension. ∎

Atomic Bomb

An early name for nuclear weapons, an atomic bomb is vastly more powerful than conventional bombs of the same size. Atomic blasts create devastating shock waves and release deadly radiation that lasts long afterwards.

The explosion results from the power released by the splitting of the nuclei of certain heavy elements, such as plutonium or uranium. Atomic—also termed nuclear—bombs are usually designed to be dropped by aircraft or delivered by guided missiles.

The first atomic bomb was built in the United States during **World War II** (1939–45) under the top-secret code-name, "Manhattan Project." On August 6, 1945, a United States B-29 bomber dropped a single atomic bomb on the Japanese city of Hiroshima, and on August 9 Nagasaki was also bombed. The Hiroshima fireball had a ground temperature of 6,000 degrees Celsius, and caused more than 140,000 casualties. Nagasaki suffered 80,000 casualties. In both cities several hundred thousand more became seriously ill from radiation poisoning. Japan immediately surrendered unconditionally.

Other nations—such as Great Britain, France, the Soviet Union, India, and Pakistan —developed their own atomic bombs, but nuclear weapons were not used again in the 20th century. ∎

ASSAULT RIFLE

In World War I (1914–18), the machine gun with its overwhelming fire power dominated infantry tactics. The infantryman needed a weapon with greater firepower, and the self-loading subma-chine gun of World War II (1939–45) was one of the first. The submachine gun was then improved upon by the German machine pistol, called *Sturmgewehr*, an "assault weapon." With a magazine of 30 rounds, the assault rifle delivers a heavy volume of fire within a range of 300 yards.

Adjustable for semi-automatic or auto-matic fire, the U.S. M16 assault rifle and the Russian Kalashnikov have become the standard infantry weapons in most armies.

U.S. M16

B

B-17 Bomber

One of the first heavy bombers of the American Air Force, the B-17 was known as the "Flying Fortress" because it carried 10 or more 50-caliber machine guns for repelling enemy fighter planes.

These four-engined bombers, based in Britain during **World War II** (1939–45), went into action with the Eighth Air Force, bombing Germany early in 1942. Flying Fortresses were fast, reaching speeds of 295-mph, and had a range of 1,100 miles. They were equipped with newly developed bombsights and **radar** that zeroed in on ground targets even in bad weather.

B-17s usually flew in close formation to help protect one another against enemy fighters. The speed and armament of Flying Fortresses and their ability to fly above 30,000 feet made it possible for them to go on missions during daylight. This enabled bombardiers to see their objectives and improve bombing accuracy.

As World War II progressed and enemy fighter tactics became more effective, losses to B-17 formations were severe. Despite the losses the B-17 payloads—3 tons of 300-pound bombs—wreaked enormous destruction to German industrial and military centers. B-17 bombers were essential to the final victory of the Allies. ■

B-2 Spirit Bomber

The four-engine B-2 is termed a "stealth" bomber because of its top-secret design and innovative technologies that make it difficult for **radar** and anti-aircraft systems to detect and track.

The B-2, which has only two crew members, a pilot and co-pilot, first went into combat in the Serbia and Kosovo bombing campaign of late 1999. Also called "a flying wing," the B-2 flies at high altitudes with a range that encompasses the entire planet. In attacks on Afghanistan in late 2001, B-2 bombers carrying as many as 80 bombs weighing 500 lbs. each flew nonstop more than 40 hours from their home base in Missouri. On their return, they landed on the island of Diego Garcia in the Indian Ocean. From there, a fresh crew flew the aircraft home. The engines were not shut down for at least 70 hours, proof of the B-2's reliability.

To achieve near-invisibility on radar, the B-2 has a pinpoint tip to its tapered nose, and is designed with flat, ultra-smooth surfaces, with no rivets showing, and every crease and crack eliminated. This "stealth bomber" even has special paint that enhances its stealth characteristics—paint that must be restored after every mission. Each B-2 costs more than $2 billion to build, making it the most expensive aircraft in history. ■

Balkan Wars

The many nationalities of the Balkans have waged bitter war with one another since the time of the ancient Greeks. Religious

B-2 REFUELING IN FLIGHT
A tanker aircraft links its fuel-delivery system to a B-2 long-range bomber, which is on a mission that takes it around the world without shutting down its engines.

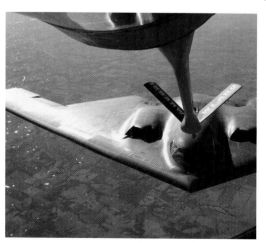

wars combined with the migrations of peoples have instilled deep hostility among ethnic Serbs, Albanians, Turks, Croats, and Greeks.

The Ottoman Empire dominated the Balkans until late in the 1800s, when successful uprisings created small nation states, each vying for security and territory. By **World War I** (1914–1918), Turkey had little influence on her former Balkan empire, which was mainly populated by Greek Orthodox Serbs and Greeks, Roman Catholic Croats, and Muslim Albanians. The aging Austro-Hungarian empire adjacent to the Balkans was the most powerful neighbor and often interfered politically in Balkan affairs. Russia also intervened, seeking Greek Orthodox allies in the Balkans and hoping to acquire a friendly warm-water seaport in the region.

Two Balkan wars took place early in the 20th century—the first, in 1912, pitting Serbia, Bulgaria, Greece, and Montenegro against Turkey, which was defeated by 1913. In 1913, a second war involved Serbia, Greece, and Romania against Bulgaria, which had made claims to Macedonian territory. Bulgaria was defeated, and peace was made.

Threats from Austria-Hungary against Serbia led to friction that deepened into all-out war when Austrian archduke Francis Ferdinand was assassinated by a Serb in Sarajevo. Entangling alliances brought Russia into the crisis on the Serbian side, and European nations honoring their military treaties lined up behind the contestants, tumbling unstoppably into World War I. ∎

Barbarian Invasions of Rome

In the 5th and 6th centuries AD, tribes from the north invaded the Western Roman Empire, which included parts of France, Italy, much of Switzerland, sections of the Balkans, and most of the North African coast. The Romans called these invading tribes "barbarians," meaning peoples from outside Roman civilization.

Among the invaders were the Goths, Visigoths, and Vandals, who had studied Roman military arts and were a match for the **legions** on the battlefield. Although considered barbarians, these peoples often had been integrated into the Roman empire and culture but now were on the move for conquest. The Western Roman Empire was in the hands of great landowners, was weighed down by heavy taxation, and could not defend itself when the invaders appeared in force.

Several barbarian kingdoms were established inside the former empire, including that of the Vandals in North Africa and the Visigoths in Spain and Gaul (now France). Roman law continued in effect in the conquered regions, and Latin was used in administration. The barbarians and Roman citizens lived in a state of coexistence. Barbarian chieftains warred among themselves for supremacy while a Roman emperor continued nominally to rule. Then, in 476, the last Roman emperor—Romulus Augustulus—was deposed by the German chief Odoacre, who named himself king—ending the Roman Empire of the West. ∎

Barbed Wire

Steel wire with points, "barbs," every few inches was strung across battlefields to protect defensive works and to hinder attacking troops. Also known as entanglement wire

BARBED WIRE BARRIER
Almost-impassable barbed wire protects World War I German entrenchments, viewed from French positions just a few yards away.

B

and anti-intrusion wire, barbed wire used in combat is termed "warwire." Barbed wire was developed in the U.S. in the mid-1800s to fence off grazing lands.

It came into military use in the **Boer War** (1899–1902), when the British strung it across the South African plains to slow the movement of raiding Boer horsemen. In **World War I** (1914–18), hundreds of miles of "No-man's Land" between opposing armies bristled with barbed wire fences laid by both armies. Machine guns so slaughtered troops struggling in barbed wire that infantry often refused to attack through barbed wire fences that had not been cut or destroyed. Artillery bombardments were laid down on barbed wire to open the way for assaults, or tanks rolled over the wire, flattening it for the infantry to cross. ■

Battleship

For almost a century, from the mid-1860s to **World War II** (1939–45), the mightiest vessel of the world's navies was the battleship, with its great naval guns, thick armored sides, and formidable cruising range.

French and British **ironclads** built in the 1850s were the first battleships. By the 1890s, the battleship was the largest and mightiest vessel on the ocean. In the final years before **World War I** (1914–18), several nations raced to construct the most powerful and fastest battleships, with the British "Dreadnought" appearing in 1906. By the outbreak of war, Britain had 73 battleships and lighter battlecruisers, while Germany had 52.

Battleships were intimidating, but they seldom joined in full-scale engagements during World War I. Even larger, faster, and more heavily armed battleships were built for World War II, with Germany's *Bismarck* as one of the most celebrated. The Americans and Japanese launched the largest battleships, with Japan's Yamato class as the largest of all time.

Air power spelled the doom of battleships. The Japanese surprise air strike on Pearl Harbor showed the vulnerability of even the mightiest warships. The *Bismarck* was crippled by air attack, and then surrounded and sunk by the British Navy. The next queen of the high seas would be the **aircraft carrier**—powerful and swift floating

BATTLESHIP ON PATROL Painted with camouflage colors, the mighty American battleship USS *New Jersey* cruises with other combat ships in World War I.

air bases that carried dozens of fighter planes, and later **helicopters,** into action around the world. ∎

Blitzkrieg

Literally "lighting war," this is a German term for a sudden attack that employs speed, surprise, superiority in firepower and overwhelming numbers. The *blitzkrieg* tactics Nazi Germany used against Poland in 1939 and against the western European Allies in 1940 combined coordinated land and air assaults. Powerful armored attacks had close dive-bomber support, smashing a hole in the enemy defenses and allowing armor and motorized infantry to pour through to cut off large pockets of defenders. The *blitzkrieg* became the accepted tactic of future conventional (not guerrilla) warfare. ∎

Boer War

Also known in Britain as the South African War and in South Africa as the Second War of Freedom, this conflict pitted the mighty British Empire against two small Boer Republics in southern Africa. Boer, in Dutch, means farmers, which a large portion of the native-born whites of southern Africa called themselves.

The South African Republic and the Orange Free State fought Britain from 1899 to 1902 over control of the gold and diamond regions inside the republics. Britain used the pretext that the Boers refused to recognize the civil rights of foreigners who came to their republics to prospect or work in the mining boom towns. The South African War followed an earlier, smaller war between the Boer republics and the British in 1880–81, which resulted in the independence of the republics.

British imperial interests wanted the mineral riches of the republics, while the Boers were fiercely independent and determined to remain so. In the first phase, Boers attacked British colonies in the region, and Boers within the colonies rebelled against British rule. The Boer fighting force—made up of 88,000 civilian volunteers—was victorious at first, but it was eventually overwhelmed by vastly superior numbers as the British sent 500,000 soldiers into the conflict.

The 1902 peace treaty took away the independence of the Boer republics and integrated them into a new state called the Union of South Africa. ∎

Bolívar, Simón (1783–1830)

South America's greatest soldier-statesman, Bolívar led the wars of liberation that freed six Latin American states from Spanish colonial rule. Born into an aristocratic Venezuelan family, Bolívar was influenced by notions of liberty and revolution during visits to the United States and Europe. He belonged to an independence movement that crossed many Latin American boundaries, and in 1811 he was influential in Venezuela's declaration of independence.

Military defeats temporarily broke up the revolutionary forces, and Bolívar rallied an army in New Granada (Colombia), reoccupying Venezuela in 1813. Again he was defeated by the Spanish royalist forces and fled to Haiti, where he reorganized and

SAVING BOER GUNS
Boer artillerymen dash away to keep their guns from capture at the Battle of Paardeberg, won by the British in 1900 during the Boer War.

B BOW & ARROW

Japan's legendary 12th-century archer, Minamoto no Tametomo, was famous for his skillful archery and for the great size of his bow.

A ca.1585 American native chief from the southeastern coast carries a bow and a quiver of arrows.

Used as long ago as the Stone Age, the bow and arrow were essential military weapons until the 16th century, when firearms gained supremacy. In Asia, the bow and arrow continued in military use for many more decades. In the Americas, most native warriors stopped using the bow by the early 1700s, favoring instead the firearms that became available through trade.

Among the most effective warrior archers were those on horseback, who could charge in and fire then gallop away before the enemy infantry could get at them. The invading Mongol hordes won many a victory in this way, surrounding an army and inflicting terrible casualties by showers of arrows.

The English longbowmen were among the most feared archers of the 13th–14th centuries, firing several hundred yards, and with deadly accuracy within 220 yards. The six-foot tall English **longbow** had the power to drive an arrow through oak doors three and a half inches thick from a distance of 220 yards.

The invention of the more powerful crossbow made the arrow—the bolt, in the crossbow's case—even more devastating to armor, thus diminishing the fighting ability of **knights** and men-at-arms. Some crossbows were large war machines that shot burning wads into fortifications under siege in order to start fires.

Early 19th-century Central Asian warriors fighting for the Czar: a Kirghiz, left, carries bow and musket; the Bashkir has a bow and a quiver of arrows.

Genoese crossbowmen, left, engage English longbow archers in the Hundred Years' War of the 14th–15th centuries.

returned to lead the revolution in New Granada. By 1819, Bolívar triumphed and was elected president of New Granada. He led campaigns to liberate Venezuela in 1821 and Ecuador a year later. Peru was liberated by 1824, followed by Upper Peru in 1825—renamed Bolivia in his honor.

Bolívar was president for life of Colombia, Peru, and Bolivia, but during the last years of his life all his efforts at uniting these states into one country failed. ■

Bonaparte, Napoleon (1769–1821)

A Corsican by birth, Napoleon Bonaparte rose through the military ranks during the French Revolution, took command of the army, and in 1804 had himself crowned as emperor.

Napoleon led France against a powerful coalition headed by Great Britain, Austria, and Russia during an era of conflict from 1796–1814. This struggle came to be called the **French Revolutionary** and **Napoleonic Wars**. In 1796–97, Napoleon was victorious in Italy and against Austria, but failed in overly ambitious expeditions to the Middle East in 1798–99.

A coup in 1799 made Napoleon military dictator of France. He won his greatest victory at Austerlitz in 1805, against the allied forces of Austria and Russia. Napoleon's success was due, in large part, to his dedicated revolutionary army with its excellent officers and outstanding generals. By 1810, his forces controlled much of Europe, but in 1812 he failed catastrophically in his invasion of Russia, losing more than half a million

men. Napoleon's empire began collapsing, and in 1814 Paris fell. He was exiled to the island of Elba, off the coast of Italy.

The next year, Napoleon returned to France and rallied his enthusiastic supporters to renew the conflict against the Allies. Final defeat came at Waterloo at the hands of forces led by the British and Prussians. Napoleon was again exiled, this time to St. Helena, an island in the South Atlantic Ocean from which he never escaped. ■

Boxer Uprising

This was a broad-based rebellion against foreign settlements in eastern China in 1899–1901. The main uprising was defeated with the capture of Beijing (Peking) by an expeditionary force of Europeans in August 1900.

Leading the Chinese attacks against foreigners was the "Society of Righteous Harmonious Fists," a nationalistic organization nicknamed "Boxers" by Westerners. Boxers murdered missionaries and their converts, and struck at foreign legations and commercial interests. The insurgents were

THE EMPEROR AS GENERAL Napoleon Bonaparte observes troop movements by telescope during his decisive 1809 victory against the Austrians at Wagram, which resulted in the surrender of Austria.

CHINESE PATRIOTS Soldiers of China's "Society of Righteous Harmonious Fists," known as "Boxers," walk a street in Tienjin during the Boxer Rebellion against foreigners in 1901. Although Western newspapers called the Boxers murderers because they killed European and American civilians as well as Chinese Christians, the Boxers believed they were patriots fighting for national liberty. Until then, foreign governments had ordered the Chinese to obey or be attacked. The Boxers objected to this and fought, unsuccessfully, to drive out the foreigners.

B

Byzantine Empress Zoe, who reigned 1028–50, was the daughter and successor of Emperor Constantine VIII; Zoe's portrait is a mosaic, made by laying in pieces of colored glass, stone, and other materials. This mosaic is in a museum in Istanbul Turkey. Byzantine influence in the Middle East and Europe lasted more than another century until the empire's capital, Constantinople—later called Istanbul by the Turks —was plundered by Western crusaders early in 1200.

secretly supported by the Chinese imperial house, whose soldiers stood aside during the uprising. The Chinese rioters resented foreign influence and economic tyranny, and attempted to drive the foreigners from their soil. In response, troops from British, French, American, German, Russian, and Italian ships were landed, and cooperated with Japanese naval forces to march on Beijing and rescue Christians besieged there. This relief force, numbering 18,700 foreign troops, marched 80 miles to the city and fought its way in to the besieged defenders.

During the following year, the Boxers were soundly defeated by several punitive expeditions of mainly German and Russian troops. Boxer leaders were punished, and the foreigners were paid reparations, and allowed to resume their business operations in China. ■

Byzantine Wars

The Byzantine Empire was also known as the Eastern Roman Empire, and came into being in 395 with the death of Roman emperor Flavius Theodosius I. The late emperor's two sons succeeded him, one ruling the western empire and one the eastern. In 474, the eastern empire became known as the Byzantine Empire, named for the original Greek colony, Byzantium, which grew to become the capital city of Constantinople. The Byzantine Empire included portions of southern and eastern Europe, western Asia, and northern Egypt.

The glittering city of Constantinople, dominating the Bosporus straits that separate Europe and Asia Minor, was the heart of a great seafaring trade and possessed a powerful fleet. For many centuries, Constantinople was the much-sought prize of invading armies, including Persians, Bulgars, Catholic crusaders, Germans, Huns, Russians, Slavs, Arabs, Seljuq Turks, and Ottoman Turks. Most of them failed in their attempts to take Constantinople.

Not only were the Byzantines a great sea power, but their armies were constantly

at war, whether defending the northern boundaries along the Danube, fighting with the Persians to the east, or engaging hordes of mounted invaders, such as the Huns, from the eastern steppelands. Byzantine forces were constantly battling Arab pirates in the Mediterranean and fending off attacks against imperial possessions in Italy.

Some Byzantine emperors sent out expeditions for conquest, but most of the Byzantine wars were fought to defend the empire. Constantinople came under siege more than once, and there were desperate occasions when the city offered tribute to approaching enemies in order to avoid yet another siege.

The Byzantine Empire was reduced to the size of a small state by 1204, when the Fourth **Crusade** captured and plundered Constantinople, and Western leaders divided up the empire. After a variety of rulers and conquerors over the succeeding two centuries, Constantinople finally fell to the Ottoman Turks in 1453, ending the Byzantine Empire. ■

EMPEROR OF BYZANTIUM Emperor Theodosius I and soldiers are seen in this detail from a votive platter commemorating the 10th anniversary of his 4th-century reign.

Caesar, Julius (100–44BC)

The greatest general of the Roman Empire, a dictator and statesman, Julius Caesar won fame as a youth when he was captured by pirates. He arranged his ransom, was freed, and then organized a naval expedition that captured the pirates, executing them by crucifixion. Caesar soon afterwards raised a private army to fight on Rome's behalf, and eventually was elected to the high Roman office of military tribune, or commander.

Starting his career in what is now Portugal, Caesar rose steadily in Roman imperial administration, participating in successful political conspiracies. His military exploits into Gaul brought him and his soldiers great profits, winning the allegiance of his followers. Caesar married into a leading Roman family, his influence and connections bringing him the governorship of Gaul, the vast region north and west of Italy.

Between 58 and 50BC, Caesar conquered lands up to the Rhine, defeating the peoples one by one. He kept a journal of these triumphs, eventually published as the military classic, *On The Gallic War*. Triumphs in Gaul and elsewhere brought Caesar fame and dynamic influence with the military, making him one of Rome's most powerful leaders. Civil strife and intrigues brought on civil war between Caesar and his political enemies. This struggle was fought throughout the empire, and as far away as Egypt, where Caesar found an ally and mistress in Queen Cleopatra.

By 48BC, Julius Caesar was sole dictator of Rome, although he was sometimes drawn away by campaigns to put down opposition in distant lands. Caesar's dictatorship was short-lived, for in the year 44BC he was assassinated in Rome by a conspiracy of political enemies. ■

Castle

The castle as a fortified stronghold developed in 9th century Europe. In medieval times, the castle was generally built upon high ground and surrounded by a ditch full of water, called a moat. By the 13th century, Western Europe had thousands of castles, erected to protect against enemy invasion. The attackers might be a nobleman leading a conquering army, or a large band of robbers plundering the countryside.

Moats were crossed by drawbridges that were raised in times of threat. Another wall, called a barbican, protected the castle's main gate, which had heavy oaken doors and iron grillwork barriers called portcullises. Masonry walls and towers surrounded the main courtyard and buildings of the castle, and upon them stood archers and fighting men. Defenders could fire from high above on attackers trying to force their way through the gate.

The central strongpoint in the castle was the keep, or dungeon (*donjon*, in French), where the defenders

LOOMING TOWERS
The high-walled 14th-century castle of Fort La-Latte in Brittany, France, endured several sieges. In ruins by the 16th century, it was reconstructed by 1715.

C

British 15th Hussars and the 1st Punjab Cavalry, a colonial regiment, engage Afghan horsemen in a 1879 battle of the Second Anglo-Afghan War.

Redcoated British dragoons fight American cavalry in the January 1781 Battle of Cowpens, won by the Americans, who were led by General Daniel Morgan.

A U.S. cavalryman on patrol in the American West ca. 1875

CAVALRY

Fighters mounted on horseback were once the key military arm for shock tactics, scouting, and speed of maneuver. Until mechanization of infantry and the development of armored vehicles and air power in the 20th-century, cavalrymen with bows, lances, and swords were essential to every army in the field.

For many centuries, the massed cavalry charge was used effectively against infantry caught in the open and was one of the most spectacular aspects of warfare. The Mongol invasions from Asia in the 11th century brought thousands of the world's finest horsemen, most of them archers, against European armies that were outmatched in speed and maneuverability.

Generals also depended on cavalry to observe enemy movements, to raid behind enemy lines, and to clear away opposing cavalry on their own scouting missions.

By the mid-19th century, however, the cavalry charge was becoming useless against the firepower of infantry and artillery. Cavalry remained important for reconnaissance until **World War I,** when aircraft took over observation and attacks behind enemy lines.

British 10th Hussars charge French cavalry in 1809 at Benavente, Spain, in the Napoleonic Wars.

and civilians could make a stand if the outer works were captured. Castles usually could hold out longer than a besieging army could stay in the field, but by the mid-1400s they became vulnerable to cannons that blasted down walls and gates. Later fortresses were designed with low walls to accommodate artillery. ∎

Chariot

The wheeled chariot first appeared in ancient Mesopotamia around 3,000BC, with a two-wheeled version becoming favored for war. The two-wheeled vehicle, drawn by two or four horses, offered speed and maneuverability in battle.

The chariot revolutionized warfare with its ability to carry fighting men into battle swiftly. Warriors on the racing chariot fought with spears and bows and also dismounted to fight on foot. For centuries, the chariot was used from Asia Minor to Egypt and the western reaches of Europe, including the British Isles.

By the era of **Alexander the Great** (356–323BC), faster-moving cavalry had superseded war chariots, although the two-wheeled vehicle remained popular for hunting and racing teams of as many as 10 horses. ∎

Charlemagne (742–814)

King of the Franks from 768 until his death, Charlemagne conquered most of the Christian lands of western Europe and ruled as emperor after 800. His name, which is French, means Charles the Great. He conquered and Christianized pagan nations such as the Saxons, and allied with the Roman Catholic pope in Rome, who wanted a powerful emperor to rule western Europe.

Charlemagne triumphed in campaigns in Spain, Hungary, and northern Italy, and his leadership and bearing made him the ideal image of the Christian ruler. The Roman church wished to become independent of the eastern Catholic Church of the Byzantine Empire. The powerful king Charlemagne was a key to their aspirations. He considered himself the feudal lord over the Catholic Church, but also believed he was responsible to God for the well-being of the Christians in his domains.

When the Saxons rebelled after having been converted, Charlemagne dealt harshly with them, executing thousands for both treason and for betraying their faith. Since the last decades of the Roman Empire four centuries earlier, no European leader had conquered and unified so great a region as Charlemagne. ∎

Chinese Civil War

The struggle of the Chinese people to create a republic started in 1926 and continued through **World War II** until 1949, when the Communists were victorious.

Early 20th-century attempts to establish a republican government under nationalist Sun Yat-sen were unsuccessful because powerful warlords dominated regions of China, raising private armies and seeking their own independence. The rise of the Communist Party, which at first allied with

GOLDEN RULER Charlemagne is portrayed as emperor of Catholic Europe in this 1349 gold and silver bust preserved in Aachen, Germany.

CATAPULT
This pre-Roman "engine of war," as early military mechanisms such as battering rams and siege towers were termed, hurled stones or fired spears and arrows. Catapults were ancient and medieval artillery. Romans termed mechanisms that fired stones, *ballista*, and those that shot arrows and spears, *catapaulta*. Their power came from the sudden release of tension on twisted cords of rope. The catapult principle continues in use in modern times to launch aircraft, especially from carriers. These systems are generally powered by hydraulic pressure.

C CHEMICAL & BIOLOGICAL WEAPONS

This World War I scene was posed in France by the U.S. Engineer Corps to illustrate the deadly effects of phosgene gas on soldiers without masks.

American soldiers in 1999 military exercises wear full protective suits for chemical and biological warfare.

World War II German poison gas warfare gear; most soldiers carried gas masks in the war, but poison gas was not used in combat.

World War I gas mask.

Chemical weapons are designed to kill or injure the enemy, and also as defoliants, to destroy the crops that serve as food and clear forests that provide cover and shelter to an enemy. The chemicals can be delivered in shells fired from cannons, by sprays from aircraft, and by bombs.

World War I (1914–18) saw the early use of poison gas—mustard gas and phosgene—against troops, mainly in the trench warfare of northwestern Europe. The invention of gas masks kept gas attacks from being decisive in World War I, and after the war, chemical weapons were outlawed by international agreement (the Geneva protocol, 1925). They were seldom used in **World War II** (1939–45). Defoliants were widely employed by American forces during the **Vietnam War** (1961–73), destroying forests and poisoning farmland, and at the same time bringing illness to civilians and soldiers alike.

By the 21st century, lethal gases such as the nerve gases sarin and tabun were in military arsenals. These attack the central nervous system. Stockpiles of chemical weapons exist in the arsenals of the United States, France, and the former Soviet Union, and also in smaller, well-armed nations such as Israel, Egypt, and Iraq.

Biological—or bacterial—warfare is the use of germs or other infecting agents to bring about illness and death. Although produced in World War II, biological agents were banned by international agreement because of their potential for wreaking widespread disaster. The most dangerous of these are anthrax and smallpox. Classified research into biological weapons continued, however, and these "weapons of mass destruction" are believed to be stockpiled in a number of nations, including the United States and the former Soviet Union.

Sun Yat-sen, subdued many warlords, but ended with bitter civil war between Nationalists under Chiang Kai-shek and the Communists led by Mao Ze Dong. These two rival regimes fought each other as well as the Japanese army, which had invaded Manchuria in 1931.

In 1934–35, Chiang's anti-communist campaigns drove Mao's forces into the mountains, the grueling retreat known as "The Long March."

The Communists regrouped and returned to conduct a guerrilla war against the Japanese in the **Sino-Japanese War**, (1937–45), and also against the Chinese Nationalists. With the defeat of Japan, the civil strife resumed, as the United States supported Chiang and the Soviet Union backed Mao.

By late 1948, the Nationalist army had been shattered, and in January 1949 Beijing fell to the Communists. That October, the Communists founded the People's Republic of China, and Chiang Kai-shek retreated to the island of Formosa to establish the Republic of China. ■

Coast Guard

Originating in the 1700s as a naval force to prevent smuggling, coast guards enforce maritime laws and assist vessels that are in distress. Many countries have such military organizations that patrol the coasts and carry out other responsibilities. These might be the rescue of shipwrecked vessels and crews, ice-breaking, preserving lighthouses, observation of icebergs, and also weather forecasting. Some of these countries also have volunteer lifeboat associations that go to the rescue of

distressed vessels along the coast. Coast guard personnel sometimes take part in overseas military operations, manning coastal and estuary patrol vessels in dangerous situations.

During wartime, coast guard operations are coordinated with the larger military effort, and duties include submarine watches along the nation's shoreline as well as the security of bays and coastal waterways. ■

Concentration Camps

These are centers for internment of individuals whom the state has deemed a threat to security, or because they are members of a particular ethnic or political group.

The internees in a concentration camp have not been lawfully found guilty of a crime, nor are they prisoners of war, but they have been confined because of the arbitrary decision of the authorities. In time of war, concentration camps are often used to prevent civilians from aiding the enemy.

The most notorious concentration camps were those of Nazi Germany, established in the mid-1930s to confine political opponents and minorities—especially Jews—who were deemed enemies of the state. The Nazis ultimately imprisoned as many as 26 million people in concentration camps,

COAST GUARD STALWART The 13,000-ton U.S. Coast Guard icebreaker *Polar Sea* has crossed the Arctic Ocean and circumnavigated Antarctica, and in 1994 became the first American surface ship to reach the geographic North Pole. This vessel, which can ram through 21 feet of ice, accommodates two helicopters and provides laboratories and sleeping quarters for up to 20 scientists.

C COMMUNICATIONS

The heraldic devices on this knight's flag and shield tell friend and foe alike whose side he is on.

A ca. 1870s Russian signal crew sends a coded message by flashing a beacon light.

German field telephone of World War II required soldiers to lay wires across the battlefield, often under enemy fire.

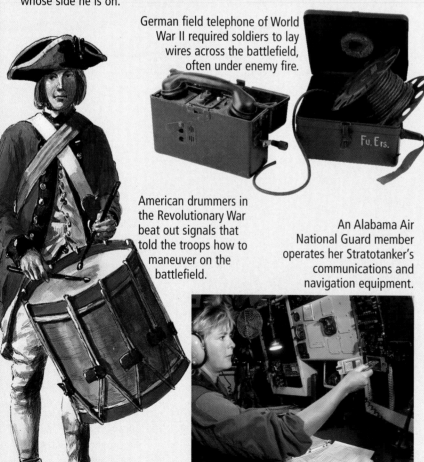

American drummers in the Revolutionary War beat out signals that told the troops how to maneuver on the battlefield.

An Alabama Air National Guard member operates her Stratotanker's communications and navigation equipment.

A military force relies on communications before and during the battle to carry out orders and learn about changes in those orders. Good communications are essential to the cooperation of the various elements of a military force.

For centuries, flags and standards carried into battle communicated the position of various units to commanders who occupied high ground to observe the battlefield. The shrill of trumpets and beating of drums also sent signals that rose above the battlefield's din to tell soldiers and officers what to do.

Communications across long distances are also crucial, and in the 1800s a system of flag signals, termed semaphore, conveyed messages to observers watching through telescopes and reading the code. Other methods included flashing sunlight in code off a mirror, and Indian warriors used smoke signals to send information. By the mid-1800s, the telegraph's Morse code offered almost instant communication of short messages. In the 20th century, field telephones communicated over a wire laid across the battlefield.

By mid-century, military communications relied on wireless radios, and later on television, with the signals bounced off satellites. Modern technology allows instant communication almost anywhere in the world.

American troops in World War II communicated by wireless "walkie-talkies," often using a decoding machine to interpret coded messages.

where millions were systematically murdered or starved to death.

The Soviet Union's concentration camps for political prisoners were comparable in cruelty. The Soviet internees usually were accused of subversion against the state.

Established by the early 1920s, some of the Soviet concentration camps—termed Gulags—continued in operation in remote areas such as Siberia as late as 1989. ■

Conquistador

The Spanish term for "conquerors"—conquistadores—was bestowed on Spain's adventurous military leaders who established their country's colonial empire in the Americas.

During the 16th century, conquistador Hernán Cortés defeated and virtually obliterated the Aztec empire of Mexico, and Francisco Pizarro took control of the Inca Empire of Peru. Both conquistadors led small forces of Spaniards, who made alliances with native peoples during their campaigns.

Spanish armor, horses, and firearms were key elements in victories over the Aztecs and Incas, whose great numbers of courageous warriors were armed only with swords, axes, spears, and bows. ■

Crimean War

Arising from disputes over control of Palestine and its Christian holy places, the Crimean War pitted Russia against the combined armies of Great Britain, France, Ottoman Turkey, and Sardinia-Piedmont.

Russia demanded the right to protect Greek Orthodox Catholics against the authority of the Muslim Turkish empire. Turkey controlled much of the Middle East, including the sacred city of Jerusalem. The French and British came to her support to prevent the Russians from gaining a warm-water seaport that opened into the Mediterranean Sea.

The war lasted from late 1853 until early 1856, and was fought mainly on the Crimean Peninsula, which juts into the Black Sea. Fighting also occurred in Romania, as Russia tried unsuccessfully to advance southward against Turkey. There were also some battles on the Black Sea.

The main allied armies landed on the southwestern tip of the Crimean Peninsula and took the port city of Sevastopol. Major engagements were fought at Alma, Balaklava, and Inkerman. The struggle was inconclusive, however, and a peace agreements was signed in February 1856. Each side lost about 250,000 soldiers, most

INTO THE "VALLEY OF DEATH"
"The Charge of the Light Brigade" is one of history's most famous cavalry attacks, as British lancers galloped across low ground raked by Russian artillery in the 1854 Crimean War Battle of Balaklava; despite heavy losses in this "Valley of Death," the lancers reached the enemy guns, only to be driven back again.

C

men succumbing to disease. Among the most enduring legacies of the war were the doomed charge of the British Light Brigade of cavalry at Balaklava and the visionary nursing work of Englishwoman Florence Nightingale. Thanks to Nightingale, new standards were set for maintaining the health of soldiers on campaign. ■

Cruise Missiles

Operating like pilotless aircraft, cruise missiles use aerodynamics rather than ballistics to reach their target. Carrying explosive warheads, cruise missiles can fly more than 1,500 miles with extreme accuracy.

Ballistic missiles are fired by rockets, "thrown" at a target, and often rise hundreds of miles into space before descending. Cruise missiles are designed to use aerodynamic lift, like an aircraft, to fly toward the target.

Guided by computer systems, the cruise missile can be air-launched from an aircraft or fired from land bases, mobile launching units, or vessels at sea, including submarines. ■

CRUSADER'S GREAT HELM

For three centuries, the "great helm," or helmet, protected those medieval fighting men who were wealthy enough to afford to own one. This helmet is made of steel, with brass reinforcing bands that end in the popular design of the *fleur-de-lis*, the "flower of the lily." It was worn over a padded cloth headpiece, and sometimes with a cowl of chain mail. Although this helmet was effective, the flat top was too vulnerable to the blows of the heavy weapons then in use. Later helmets had rounded or conical crowns to more easily ward off blows from above.

Crusades

Beginning in 1091 and for the next 200 years, mobs of armed European Christians journeyed to the Middle East to attack the Muslim states that controlled the Holy Land, as Palestine, Syria, Jordan, and Lebanon were known.

At least seven expeditions—termed "crusades" because the participants made vows upon the Christian cross and were endorsed by the Roman church—invaded the Middle East between the 11th and 13th centuries.

Cities on the route of crusader armies were often brutally attacked and pillaged, with hundreds of thousands slaughtered. One crusade even sacked Constantinople, which was the seat of Greek Orthodox Christianity.

The invaders sought to establish their own states and make the land associated with Christ and Biblical times wholly Christian. The crusaders at first dominated the region and several "crusader states" were established, including one state at Jerusalem, the holiest city of the Christians and the Jews.

Muslim peoples fought back, however, and with increasing success. One by one, each crusader state was overcome, and Muslim rule was again established throughout the Middle East and the Holy Lands.

A lasting bitterness has remained for centuries among the Muslims, who still consider the Crusades a great evil cruelly brought upon the Muslim peoples by fanatical European Christians. ■

FIERCE AND BLOODY CONFLICT This Italian painting shows the fury of the many pitched battles brought on by the crusader invasions of Muslim lands.

E

Egyptian-Hittite War

One of the earliest known wars, this was the clash in the 13th century BC between the Egyptians and the Hittite invaders, who were descending from the north into Syria and Palestine.

The Hittites were among the first to develop iron weapons and tools and to use **chariots** drawn by horses in battle. Later, the Egyptians developed their own battle-chariots as they conquered all southwest Asia except for Hittite-held Syria. The Egyptian victory at Kadesh, Syria, in 1288BC is the earliest recorded use of battlefield formations and tactics.

In 1271BC, the Egyptians and Hittites established an alliance that dominated the smaller states of southwest Asia for almost four centuries. ■

Eighty Years War

From 1568 until 1648, the Dutch people of the Lowlands struggled for independence from Spain. This struggle resulted in the formation of the Dutch Republic, known as the United Provinces of the Netherlands (Lowlands).

Under Prince William I of Orange, Protestant armies brought about a broad-based Dutch uprising to fight the occupying Catholic forces of Spain. The Dutch provinces united and formed a union against Spain's powerful professional army and navy, which occupied the southern Lowlands, now Belgium. When Spain became involved with conflicts against England and France, the Dutch managed to wrest themselves free of Spanish dominance.

A truce was established in 1609, but warfare resumed in 1621, with first the Spanish and then the Dutch gaining the upper hand. In 1648, after almost constant conflict, Spain at last recognized Dutch independence. ■

Eisenhower, Dwight D. (1890–1969)

As the American commander of Allied European operations in **World War II** (1939–45), General Eisenhower oversaw the invasions of Sicily and Italy in 1943. Eisenhower became Supreme Commander of the Allied Expeditionary Force for the invasion of Normandy in 1944.

Eisenhower was able to unify his senior commanders from the United States, Great Britain, and France. While coordinating military operations, he was under constant pressure from influential politicians who wanted him to follow their wishes. He led Allied forces to victory over the Axis forces in Europe in April 1945 and oversaw the final triumph against Japan in August.

After World War II, Eisenhower served as Chief of Staff of the Army and supreme commander of NATO (North Atlantic Treaty Organization) forces. He was U.S. president from 1953–61. ■

THE EVE OF D-DAY
Allied Supreme Commander Dwight Eisenhower talks to paratroopers of the American 101st Airborne, the "Screaming Eagles," as they prepare for their jump behind Nazi lines during the invasion of Normandy in June 1944.

E EDGED WEAPONS

German rapier and matching dagger (at left), are replicas of 16th century weapons.

A Union Civil War officer waves his sword, leading enlisted men who have bayonets fixed to their muskets.

Bladed weapons with a sharp cutting edge include swords and daggers, which were standard fighting gear until early in the 19th century. While firearms reigned supreme by the 18th century, cavalry and officers continued to wield swords in battle. Massed firepower and improved accuracy of firearms finally also made these swords obsolete.

From the earliest centuries BC, swords were the infantry weapon for close combat, and various types of daggers were also employed. The Roman *gladius*–short, double-edged, and with a point–was designed for thrusting. The *gladius* was extremely lethal when wielded by closely massed Roman infantry against looser enemy formations using large broadswords that required more space to swing.

Centuries later, European **knights** carried enormous swords, but when **gunpowder** and firearms began to dominate in the 16th century, swords were no longer the main weapon for the foot soldier. Swords remained the symbol of an officer's authority, and cavalrymen continued to use them in combat into the 20th century.

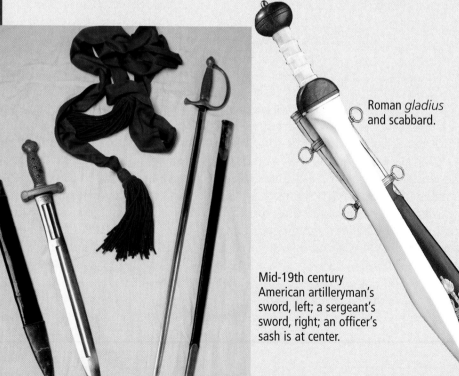

Roman *gladius* and scabbard.

Mid-19th century American artilleryman's sword, left; a sergeant's sword, right; an officer's sash is at center.

Elephants

India was using decorated and armored elephants as instruments of military terror at the time Alexander invaded that region in the 4th century BC.

Later, elephants were employed by some Greek armies on campaign. The beasts were placed in pairs along a battle-front or massed 15 or 20 together. On their backs they often carried towers that held several soldiers and the elephant trainer. The elephant's shock power in a charge was instrumental in a number of victories in the last centuries BC. Many elephants died in battle, however, and soldiers learned how to avoid their charges.

Among the most famous uses of the elephant was **Hannibal's** invasion of Rome over the Alps in 218BC, crossing rivers with his war elephants on a bridge of rafts.

For centuries, elephants continued to be used in Asia as traditional instruments of war, but were ineffective in battle against well-trained infantry and cavalry. ∎

Engineers

Military engineering involves Combat Engineering to support troops in battle and Strategic Engineering to establish communications, and build roads and fortifications. In modern warfare, military engineering includes constructing airfields, supply depots, **railroads,** and seaport facilities.

Military engineers were important even in the ancient world, and are considered the first "scientific soldiers." The hill forts of the Iron Age in Europe and the great Middle East fortresses of the Persians are examples of early civil engineering that later was brought to peacetime construction. The greatest military engineering feat of all time is the 1,500-mile **Great Wall of China,** which began construction in the 4th century BC and was still being worked on in the 16th century.

Throughout the ages, science and technology have combined in military engi-

neering to create defensive works, bridge rivers, undermine an enemy's stronghold, and plan the sites of battles to account for the many aspects of combat such as artillery fire, machine gun positions, resupply, shelter for troops, armored warfare, air combat, and guided missiles. ∎

MAJESTIC ELEPHANTS
The Rajput Army of 19th-century India used trained elephants as beasts of war and also in parades as ceremonial bearers of important personages.

English Civil War

A struggle between the royalist forces of King Charles I and the supporters of Parliament, this conflict raged in the British Isles from 1642–51. It is also called the Puritan Revolution because the religious group known as Puritans was in the majority of Parliament's forces.

The great military leader of Parliamentary armies was Oliver Cromwell, a Puritan general who led Parliament to victory in England. The king was executed in 1649, and Cromwell ruled the nation as "lord protector" as he and the Puritans attempted to establish a republican-style commonwealth.

Civil war continued in Ireland and Scotland until 1651, and no permanent settlement was reached between the Puritan-controlled state and the Anglican church, which longed for the restoration of a king. Cromwell died in 1658, and Parliament at last approved the return to the throne of Charles II, son of the executed monarch, in 1660. ∎

E

EXPLOSIVES

There are several types of explosives, including mechanical, chemical, and nuclear. In principle, explosives are substances that, when ignited, suddenly produce a great quantity of gas, often at extremely high temperatures.

Gunpowder, ignited by fire, was known in China and Southwest Asia by the 13th century, when military rockets were in use by the Arabs. In the mid-14th century, both Arabs and Europeans knew how to use gunpowder to throw projectiles from metal tubes. Gunpowder is a fine mixture of nitre, charcoal, and sulfur.

Firearms in the hands of infantry, and the development of artillery in the 15th century, decisively altered military methods. War was further changed by the development of hollow shells containing chemical explosives—high explosives—that detonated on reaching the target, causing death and destroying fortifications.

In the mid-20th century, the far more explosive power unleashed by the nuclear-fission process was harnessed in the components of a bomb that could be dropped from a plane. Later, nuclear bombs and high explosives were placed in warheads that could be delivered across thousands of miles by guided missiles.

A Union mine filled with 8,000 pounds of gunpowder explodes under Confederate fortifications at Petersburg, Virginia, in July 1864.

A Marine demolition crew watches dynamite charges destroy a Japanese cave in Okinawa, May 1945.

American artillerymen carry a 155mm shell during live fire-and-maneuver training in the Middle East in 2000.

The most destructive explosive: a hydrogen bomb detonates during a test.

Explosive Ordnance Disposal teams collected land mines, grenades, surface-to-air missiles, air-to-air missiles, and various small arms from Afghanistan's Kandahar Airport in 2001.

F

Falklands War

Although Britain has colonized the Falklands Islands in the South Atlantic since 1833, Argentina also claims ownership. The Argentines call the two windswept main islands of East and West Falkland, as well as their few dependency islands, the Malvinas.

In April 1982, the military junta ruling Argentina invaded the lightly defended Falklands, a self-governing colony. Mediation attempts by the United States and the United Nations failed, and Britain assembled an invasion force that journeyed 8,000 miles by sea and air to recapture the Falklands.

The conflict was fierce, but brief, with British sea power cutting off Argentine troops on the islands. By mid-June, Britain had captured the last Argentine positions holding out near Port Stanley, the capital. More than 11,000 Argentines surrendered, and 662 were estimated as dead or missing. The British suffered 55 killed and 777 wounded. ■

Field Cannon

Early artillery of the late 1400s was transported on ox-drawn wagons, then offloaded and set up for battle. This slow process worked for sieges but was useless for open-field battles involving infantry and cavalry.

In the **Hundred Years' War** (1337–1453) between France and England, the French began using horses to pull their cannon wagons. This offered much more speed of maneuver, helping the French win the war. By the 1600s, field cannons were set on their own wheels, which made them even more mobile.

In the **Thirty Years' War** (1618–1648), Sweden's general-king Gustavus Adolphus employed light, two-wheeled field guns that could be rushed by teams of horses into battle. Swedish guns were quickly massed to support infantry assaults or take new positions to defend against an enemy attack. Guns fired cannonballs or clusters of small iron balls called grape shot or canister, which could cut swaths through densely packed enemy troops.

With the widespread use of cannons and firearms, military tactics changed into a more open battle order, forcing infantry and cavalry to maneuver swiftly to avoid gunfire.

Field cannons remained small through the 19th century, their effective range was just a few hundred yards. Late in the 20th century, field artillery used explosive shells with fuses timed to blow up over enemy positions. In **World War I** (1914–18), field cannons hauled by horses or trucks were the most decisive arm of the war, with ranges of several thousand yards. Massed artillery bombardments forced infantry into deep bunkers and helped bring on the prolonged trench warfare of the Western Front.

Every conventional 20th century army

CHINESE GUNNERS
Chinese artillerymen stand at attention beside their old-fashioned field cannon sometime between 1900–10.

F

FIREARMS

World War II American submachine guns: top, the Thompson M1; bottom, the M3, nicknamed the "Grease Gun." Both fired .45 caliber ammunition.

Top and middle, British Lee-Enfield bolt-action rifles, showing a grenade launcher cup at top and a bayonet in the middle; bottom, U.S. M1 Garand semi-automatic, with bayonet.

Modern U.S. Army soldiers firing assault rifles during training maneuvers.

This term generally means handguns or guns with stocks that fit against the shoulder when fired.

Early firearms appeared in the 15th century. These generally were large guns that stood on platforms or mounts. Their charge of black powder **(gunpowder)** was ignited to propel various types of projectiles—stones, arrows, and later iron balls. The **musket** developed in the 1500s as the individual soldier's firearm.

At first, the slow-loading musketeer was vulnerable to a charging enemy. Further, his gun was not dependable in wet weather, which could spoil the black powder charge. Improved firing and loading methods steadily enhanced the effectiveness of muskets and pistols. By the late 1600s, they were fitted with flintlocks, which sparked flint against steel to ignite the black powder charge. This was the dominant military firearm for the next 150 years.

In the mid-19th century, percussion ignition and rifled barrels further improved the reliability, accuracy, and speed of firing. Later in the century came breechloading firearms, repeating rifles, and metallic cartridges. Through the first half of the 20th century, the infantryman's rifle was overmatched by machine guns. In later decades, the submachine gun, the machine pistol, and the assault rifle gave individual soldiers immense firepower, both in volume of fire and accuracy.

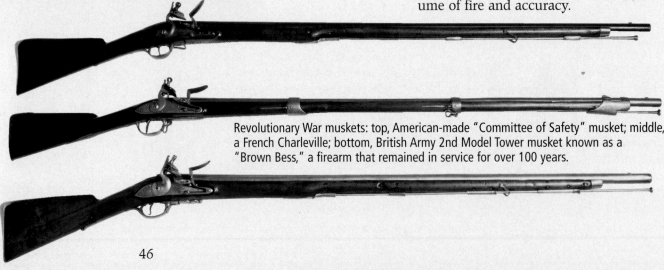

Revolutionary War muskets: top, American-made "Committee of Safety" musket; middle, a French Charleville; bottom, British Army 2nd Model Tower musket known as a "Brown Bess," a firearm that remained in service for over 100 years.

required mobile field cannons to support troop movements, pin down enemy defenders, or repel an attack.

World War II (1939–45) and the **Korean War** (1950–53) saw the mechanization of field guns, either self-propelled or towed by fast-moving trucks. ■

Flamethrower

A portable apparatus that fires a long jet of burning liquid, the flamethrower is effective against an enemy hiding inside strong defensive works. The soldier using the flamethrower must get within 20 or 30 yards of the enemy position.

Flamethrowers were first developed in **World War I** (1914–18). The basic system requires a metal tank holding a flammable liquid, such as a mixture of creosote oil and gasoline or benzene, under compressed air pressure. When the weapon is fired the liquid is ejected through a launching tube fitted with an automatic igniter. The stream of flame sears the target, scorching bunkers and caves, consuming the oxygen inside them, and setting fire to whatever can burn. ■

Franco-Mexican War

After the Mexican Civil War (1858–61), which ended in the victory of the Liberal army under Benito Juárez, French, British, and Spanish forces captured Veracruz in December 1861. The invaders claimed to be protecting their national interests, but aimed to take advantage of the American Civil War and expand their influence in the Americas.

The British and Spanish soon departed, and French troops remained to occupy Mexico. The U.S. was too embroiled in its own war to oppose this imperialism. Mexican resistance was strong, however. The French army was defeated in the Battle of Cinco de Mayo. Reinforced to 30,000, the French army captured Mexico City in June 1863 and established Archduke Maximilian of Austria as a puppet emperor of Mexico. Maximilian was an ally of the French emperor, Louis Napoleon III.

Mexican resistance continued, and the end of the American Civil War brought a final U.S. demand for a French withdrawal. The French left Mexico by early 1867, and in May the patriotic resistance defeated and captured Maximilian, who was executed. ■

FLINTLOCK
Guns with mechanisms (locks) that use a piece of flint to strike a spark and fire the weapon are flintlocks. The flintlock ignition system was introduced in the late 16th century, was universally adopted for European military firearms by 1700, and remained dominant in firearms until the middle of the 19th century. When the trigger of a flintlock is pulled, an internal spring action causes the hammer with the flint to strike sparks on the frizzen that ignite gunpowder in the priming pan. This in turn fires the main charge that shoots the ball. In the 19th century, the flintlock system was replaced by the percussion cap —small brass cups with a chemical charge that ignites upon the impact of the gun's hammer.

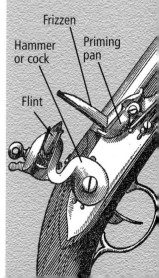

Frizzen

Hammer or cock

Priming pan

Flint

LIQUID FIRE U.S. Marines use flamethrowers against dug-in Japanese positions on Saipan in the Pacific in 1944.

F FLAGS

National flags flutter bravely as Union troops charge Confederates in the 1862 Battle of Cedar Mountain, Virginia.

Cloths bearing symbolic designs and colors and fitted on poles were used in India and China many centuries BC to indicate the identity and position of a military force.

Flags are traced back to ancient Egypt and Assyria, where a sacred object was placed on a pole to inspire soldiers or to indicate a central rallying point in battle. Roman legionnaires carried an eagle standard with their **legion's** designated number. Flags were used in battle to indicate the location of a king or the headquarters of a commander in the field. Flags also could be waved to send prearranged signals back and forth across the battlefield.

National flags were often carried by military units, such as regiments, each of which also had its own flag. Emblems and numbers on a regimental flag showed its designation in the army and also any honors it had won.

Until the end of the 19th century, flags were carried at the head of an attacking force to lead the charge, and they waved defiantly over defensive positions under attack. Modern warfare, often fought by individual soldiers scattered over a wide area, seldom involves the use of flags in battle.

English naval pennants and flags unfurl to the wind in this 16th century scene of King Henry VIII aboard the *Great Harry* with sails of gold cloth; flag signals governed the fleet's movements, with the supreme commander's "flagship" sending the key signals.

Prussian cavalrymen wave captured Austrian battle flags to honor their king, Frederick the Great, after a 1745 victory.

Russians mount their flag over captured Berlin in 1945.

Viet Minh troops signal the taking of French positions at Dien Bien Phu in 1954.

Franco-Prussian War

Prussian Chancellor Otto von Bismarck sought to unite the many German states and principalities all into one powerful empire. To do so, Bismarck conspired to draw France into a war.

The French emperor, Napoleon III, felt threatened by Bismarck's efforts to build a German empire, and by Prussian moves to influence the future of the Spanish royal house. Provoked by Bismarck's intrigues, France declared war in July 1870.

As Bismarck anticipated, the German states united, and invaded France, which was decisively defeated at Sedan in August. Paris fell in January 1871, a bitter humiliation for the French and a stimulus to the permanent unification of a greater Germany. King William I of Prussia was proclaimed emperor of the German empire, which annexed the eastern French provinces of Alsace and Lorraine.

The Franco-Prussian War prepared the way for the 20th century's two world wars, which sprang from old hatreds and the desire to avenge defeats. ∎

Franks-Moors Wars

The Christian peoples of the present France and western Germany, known as Franks, warred for many generations against the Muslims of Spain, called Moors.

In the early 8th century, Moorish armies were moving northward, threatening to conquer the Franks and eventually western Europe. A Frankish force under Charles Martel won a battle at Tours in 732, decisively stopping the Moor advance.

Martel's grandson, **Charlemagne,** continued to war with the Moors, and unsuccessfully attempted to invade Spain in 777–778.

The retreat of Charlemagne and the Franks from Spain ended the broader

GERMANY'S FOUNDER

Prussian chancellor Otto von Bismarck (1815–98) took firm control over his king and government from the 1860s to the late 1870s; he led Prussia through several victorious wars and united most German states into one country. Prussia's swift victories over Austria in 1866 and France in 1871 were largely thanks to Bismarck's abilities as a leader. Unfortunately, those wars gave Europeans the mistaken belief that modern conflicts would be quick and decisive and without much civilian suffering. World War I, with its grinding campaigns and huge losses, would prove this belief to be disastrously wrong.

PRUSSIAN *KURRASSIERS* Heavy cavalry with steel helmets and breastplates attack the French during the 1870 Franco-Prussian War. Modern breech-loading firearms were making such attacks too costly.

F FORTIFICATIONS

Jerusalem's walls and towers defied besiegers in the age of the Crusades.

Rebels dug field fortifications on Breed's Hill above Boston in 1775; British Redcoats captured the position, but at great loss.

Guarding the harbor of Charleston, South Carolina, Fort Sumter was built in a "casement" design, with the guns in protective rooms.

Defensive works and strongholds can be of masonry, built in times of peace, or earthworks and trenches that are built during wartime, while in close contact with an enemy.

Fortifications are positioned to take advantage of natural obstacles to enemy advances, such as high ground and rivers. They often are concealed and camouflaged in order to be difficult for the enemy to study while planning for an attack. Fortifications prevent the enemy from attacking through the easier routes of invasion.

Historically, most cities were fortified with walls, protected bridges, and waterways. In Roman times, **legions** on campaign built forts all along their routes of march, making it possible for an outnumbered force to defend itself while in enemy lands. Medieval **castles** were designed to endure long sieges that often wore out the enemy invaders and compelled them to withdraw. In the 17th and 18th centuries, military fortifications designed for artillery and musketry achieved a high degree of sophistication, with the military **engineer** rising to prominence in the art of war.

In the early 20th century, armies in the field dug networks of trenches to prevent enemy advances and protect the defending troops from bombardment. Later, guerrilla wars, such as in Vietnam, called for hastily constructed base camps made of earthworks reinforced with logs and sandbags. These fortifications shelter troops from unexpected mortar fire and rocket attacks.

Permanent fortifications employed in the **Arab-Israeli wars** were designed as strongpoints that could hold out against enemy assaults from the ground or air. By preventing the attacker from clearing the battlefront, such fortified strongpoints keep the advancing force distracted and under fire until a counterattack can be mounted by the defending army.

Franks-Moors conflict, but the Moors had to repulse yet another Frankish invasion of Spain early in the 9th century. ■

Frederick II, the Great (1712–86)

The third king of Prussia, Frederick forged his small country into a leading European power by developing the army and employing it with military genius that won him the title, "the Great."

Frederick modernized 18th-century warfare by the thorough and strict training of infantry and by improving his artillery. Prussian field guns became fast-moving on the battlefield and displayed devastating firepower in close support of Prussian infantry. A key to fashioning his first-rate army was Frederick's call for young Prussian noblemen to become lifelong members of the splendid officer corps. Although the tradition of the day was for European officers to remain aloof from the soldiers, Frederick's officers personally supervised the training and discipline of their men.

The result gave Prussia the best military force in Europe during Frederick's lifetime. His finest victories were during the **Seven Years' War** (1756–63) over the combined armies of France, Germany, and Austria, which vastly outnumbered the Prussians. ■

French and Indian War

This North American phase of the worldwide conflict known as the **Seven Years' War** (1756–63) was fought between the colonies of Britain and France.

The war ended a century of struggle to control the vast wilderness between New France and British America. The French had more allies among the native peoples than did the British. On the other hand, Britain had 1.5 million colonists in several prosperous colonies, while New France had only a few hundred thousand colonists.

The French and their Indian allies were victorious at first. They captured frontier forts, destroyed a British expeditionary force in what is now Pennsylvania, and

A KING AMONG HIS SOLDIERS Prussia's King Frederick the Great cheerfully greets his Bernberg infantry regiment while on a campaign. Frederick was a strict disciplinarian, but his troops adored him.

F

F

A NATION IN ARMS

Pictured are French infantry of the French Revolutionary Wars, which followed the overthrow of King Louis XVI. Under attack by the major European powers, France rallied her citizens to resist the invading armies. Amidst continual political turmoil at home, France's ragged armies of volunteers were victorious. Ambitious generals like the young Napoleon Bonaparte learned their trade during the many campaigns that saw France's armies conquer Italy and the Netherlands. Although often ill-supplied, and plagued with political overseers, the French armies of the revolutionary period set the stage for the great military successes of the Napoleonic Wars.

WOLFE DIES HAPPY Hearing the French stronghold of Quebec has fallen to his army, wounded British general James Wolfe declares, "I die happy," as his sorrowing troops, colonials, and native allies look on.

drove thousands of settlers from the interior. By late 1758, however, the tide of war had turned in Great Britain's favor. Fort Louisburg, guarding the mouth of the Saint Lawrence River, fell to the British, as did Niagara, Ticonderoga, and Crown Point. The climax came with the fall of Quebec in 1759, where British general James Wolfe died from his wounds at the moment of victory.

Final peace terms were approved in 1763, ceding Canada and a vast territory east of the Mississippi to Britain, which now was the dominant power in North America. ■

French Revolutionary Wars

After the French Revolution overthrew the Bourbon monarchy and pulled down the aristocracy in 1792, the French were inspired to carry their ideals of liberty and equality to other nations.

Considering themselves free citizens who had an obligation to enlist, the French built up armies larger than Europe had ever seen before. France became a nation in arms, with more than 700,000 troops in the 1790s. At first, many nations admired French ideals and welcomed their troops. In time, Europeans considered the French to be aggressors trying to expand their territory and power. Spain, Prussia, Russia, and Austria battled the French armies on land, and were joined by Britain, with its mighty navy.

In the late 1790s **Napoleon Bonaparte** rose to power by leading the French to successive triumphs, although British naval victories thwarted his campaigns in the Mediterranean regions. By 1799, French armies were operating on a broad front, from Italy through Switzerland to Germany and the Lowlands. In this year, Napoleon was named first consul, military dictator of France.

In 1802 Napoleon was appointed first consul for life. This marked the close of the French Revolutionary Wars.

Two years later, Napoleon became emperor, and the European conflicts of this period were known as the **Napoleonic Wars**. They ended with Bonaparte's defeat at Waterloo in 1815. ■

G

Galleon

These large sailing ships of the 15th and 16th centuries were named after the "galley," an ancient war vessel propelled by oars and with a beaked prow. Galleons incorporated this high prow design, but they were full-rigged ships with three or four masts.

The galleon had a high forecastle at the prow and carried one or two tiers of cannons along its sides. Also known as "men-of-war," galleons were the most formidable ships on the seas, sometimes carrying hundreds of soldiers for defense and for boarding enemy vessels or for attacking seaports. The largest galleons were built by Spain and Portugal. Heavily armed Spanish galleons were required each year to protect the hundreds of rich merchant vessels, laden with silver and silks, coming from Mexico or the Philippines. Many great galleons were in the **Spanish Armada,** defeated by the English in 1588. The galleons could not come to grips with the smaller, faster English warships, which were armed with long-range guns.

After the defeat of the armada, naval warfare was decided by cannon fire rather than by closing in for boarding by soldiers. The mighty galleon soon gave way to sleeker vessels designed for maneuverability and for "off-fighting" with artillery. ∎

Galley

Long, narrow ships propelled by oars, galleys were used in the Mediterranean in the days of ancient Egypt. The largest galleys had hundreds of oarsmen and also were fitted with sails. These vessels were seagoing, and could travel far.

About 700BC, the Phoenecians introduced the bireme, which had two banks of oars on each side. The trireme, with three banks of oars on each side, was designed by the Greeks around 500BC.

Galley warfare followed methods employed by armies on land, with squadrons of vessels organized in columns and lines. Opposing war galleys surged toward each other, oars dipping and rising in cadence, aiming to crash the rams on their prows into the side of the enemy ship or to shatter a bank of oars and thus disable the opponent. Grappling irons and ropes were thrown over the enemy vessel to pull it close enough for soldiers to leap across on the attack.

Many fighting men served as oarsmen, picking up weapons when the battle began.

GALLEON _VICTORIA_
In 1519, Portuguese explorer Ferdinand Magellan departed from Spain with five ships, including the galleon _Victoria;_ Magellan died on the way, but his expedition was the first to sail around the world.

G

GARAND M1 SEMI-AUTOMATIC RIFLE

This gas-operated 30-caliber rifle was the key weapon of the U.S. infantryman in World War II and the Korean War. The Garand is a "self-loader," its firing mechanism automatically removing the spent shell and placing a new bullet in the empty chamber. A spurt of gas moves the piston that powers this system, which also cocks the weapon, ready for the infantryman to pull the trigger and fire.

The magazine's eight rounds can be fired within twenty seconds. American World War II general George S. Patton called the M1 "the greatest battle implement ever devised."

U.S. M1 Garand semi-automatic rifle with bayonet

The swift Viking longships of 900–1100 were small galleys, with 10 oars on a side. Although all-sail vessels became favored by the 15th century, galleys were prominent in the European defeat of the Turkish fleet at Lepanto in 1571.

Galleys remained in use, for trade and for war, well into the 17th century, and war galleys occasionally saw action during the **French Revolutionary Wars** (1792–1802). ∎

Gallic Wars

In 58–52BC, Roman consul **Julius Caesar** led an army into Gaul in quest of riches and military glory. Gaul was the region of western Europe which is today France, Switzerland, the Lowland countries, western Germany, and northern Italy.

Caesar intended to rise in popularity above his rivals for rulership of the Roman empire, and he succeeded. His campaigns were known as the Gallic Wars, and won him fame throughout the empire. He subdued virtually all the lands he invaded–including crossing the English Channel and defeating a force of Britons. He often had to return to conquered tribes to suppress rebellions.

Victory over the great Gaulish leader, Vercingetorix, in 52BC was the final decisive triumph that won Caesar the reputation and glory he was after.

Julius Caesar recorded these exploits in his much-read book, *On the Gallic War.* ∎

Gatling Repeat Fire Gun

Although invented in the U.S. in 1862, the Gatling crank-operated, 10-barrel machine gun was little used in the Civil War because the military did not understand its potential in battle.

Improvements in cartridges after the war soon brought the Gatling gun into American military service. Manufactured by the famous Colt arms company, the Gatling gun was especially effective in the **Spanish-American War** of 1898.

Ammunition was fed to the gun from a hopper set on top of the revolving barrels, which were turned by a hand crank. When a barrel came to the top of a revolution, it received a cartridge. The barrels moved from position to position as the crank was turned, following the sequence: new bullet placed in firing chamber, breech closed, gun cocked, bullet fired, empty shell ejected, barrel reloaded.

The Gatling gun was capable of firing 800 times a minute. Modern electric-powered Gatling guns, which are mounted on specialized attack aircraft such as the A-10 Thunderbolt II, are able to fire thousands of rounds a minute. ∎

CROSSING THE RHINE Ducking for cover under heavy Nazi fire, U.S. Army soldiers cross the Rhine in an assault boat at St. Goar, Germany, March 1945. The men are armed with M1 Garand semi-automatic rifles.

UNDER FIRE ON SAN JUAN HILL American soldiers fall in a Spanish-American War engagement while their rapid-fire Gatling gun opens on enemy troops dug into San Juan Hill, Cuba.

Genghis Khan (ca.1162–1227)

With a name that means "Universal Ruler" of the Mongolian people of Central Asia's steppe lands, Genghis Khan is one of history's most famous conquerors.

Genghis Khan created a fierce and terrible army of 20,000 mounted fighters that subjugated Mongolian and Tatar peoples and forged them into a powerful fighting force. His Mongol warriors were feared and admired for their ability to fire arrows while racing on horseback around an enemy force. Mongol cavalry employed bow, lance, and scimitar. They had two types of bows and three types of arrows designed either for close fighting or for firing at a distance. No warriors could match the mounted Mongol archer for speed and skill.

Genghis Khan captured Beijing in 1215, and then his armies turned eastward to invade Persia and Russia. His Mongol Empire eventually extended to the Adriatic Sea of southern Europe, encompassing many different Christian, Muslim, and Buddhist peoples. ∎

Golden Horde

The western portion of the Mongol Empire, called the Kipchak Khanate, adopted the Muslim religion and the Turkish language by the 13th century. Mounted raiders from the Khanate, known as the "Golden Horde," went on military campaigns, capturing cities in Silesia and fighting in the Caucus Mountains to the south. The Golden Horde captured Moscow in 1382, slaughtering many inhabitants.

For decades, these warriors dominated Russia and the surrounding regions, and they warred among themselves for domination of the Khanate. In 1391, Central Asian ruler Tamerlane defeated the Khanate of the Golden Horde in the Battle of the Steppes, but elements of the Horde continued raiding. Tamerlane dealt them another defeat in 1395, but a year later the Golden Horde triumphed over an army of Poles and German **knights**. It required another century before the Golden Horde lost its power, being decisively defeated by Poles and Lithuanians in 1491. ∎

Grant, Ulysses S. (1822–85)

As commander of the Union Army in the **U.S. Civil War** from 1864–65, General Grant led federal troops in the final victory over

TWO WARRIORS
A Mongol horseman, right, engages a Mogul warrior in the ongoing conflicts that raged for hundreds of years across Central Asia and eastern Europe until the 15th century.

G

Confederate general **Robert E. Lee** in northern Virginia. Grant was appointed overall Union commander by President Abraham Lincoln, who was impressed with the former West Pointer's victories in the Mississippi River and Tennessee campaigns.

Grant drove his army relentlessly against the Confederates under Lee, often at great cost in dead and wounded lost in frontal attacks. However, his war of attrition succeeded in wearing down the enemy, who could not replace lost men and supplies as readily as the Union could.

Grant accepted Lee's final surrender at Appomattox Court House, Virginia, in April 1865, effectively ending the Civil War. He was elected 18th president of the United States in 1869, but his eight years in office were clouded by government scandals and rampant corruption. ■

Great Northern War

In 1700, when Sweden was the leading military power of Northern Europe and the Baltic Sea, an anti-Swedish coalition brought on a war that lasted until 1721, resulting in her decline.

Opposing powerful Sweden were Russia, Denmark, Norway, Saxony, and Poland. The Swedes, led by King Charles XII, were successful at first, winning battles against their enemies one by one.

Peter the Great, czar of Russia, finally defeated Charles at Poltava in 1709. This victory renewed the spirits of the other members of the coalition, and they redoubled their military efforts.

In the end, Sweden lost considerable territory along the Baltic, and Russia began her rise to power. ■

Great Wall of China

Built over the course of centuries, the Great Wall was made to protect China from invasions by roving Huns to the westward.

Parts of the wall existed as early as the 4th century BC, and 200 years later these separate sections of the wall began to be connected into one long fortification. Watchtowers and ramparts were built to protect the defending troops. Each successive Chinese dynasty increased the length of the wall.

The watchtowers, usually on high hills, held beacon fires that could send smoke signals in the daytime and the light of a fire at night. Messages were conveyed from tower to tower, eventually traveling all the way to the capital, Beijing.

The Great Wall is one of the world's largest man-made structures. It extends 1,500 miles, from the Yellow Sea on the east to the mountainous wilderness of Central Asia to the west. Made of brick in some places, and elsewhere of earthen dikes faced with masonry, the wall rises 30 feet high, with 40-foot watchtowers.

In times of banditry or warfare, the broad causeway along the top of the Great Wall served as a safe passage for travelers and commerce passing back and forth across the country. ■

Greco-Persian Wars

Between the 6th and 5th centuries BC, the Greek states engaged in a great struggle with the Persian Empire of Asia. Mighty battles on land and sea were fought over the course of 100 years, with the Greeks ultimately triumphing.

WALLS AND WATCHTOWERS
The Great Wall of China at Simatai, a few hours from Beijing; here, the wall is worn and weathered, but its imposing grandeur and former glory still can be seen.

Persian invaders were driven from Europe, and the fiercely independent Greek civilization survived. This conflict is best known for two land battles–Marathon in 490BC, and Thermopylae in 480BC–and the accompanying sea battle of Salamis.

Persian King Xerxes was defeated at Marathon by an army one fifth the size of his own. Ten years later, he won at Thermopylae and sacked Athens, but half his fleet was sunk by the Greek fleet at Salamis, forcing him to withdraw to Asia. The Greeks then went on the offensive, and the war continued for another 30 years.

By 448BC, the Persians had given up attempting to dominate the Greek states. ■

Grenade

The infantryman either throws this small fragmentation bomb or can fire it from a rifle. The grenade's explosion hurls metal slugs in all directions and is especially lethal against infantry.

Early grenades, developed in the 16th century, were hollow iron balls filled with black powder. They were fitted with a fuse that was lit just before the bomb was hurled. By the 17th century, soldiers trained to throw grenades were organized into elite companies and named "grenadiers." These men had to be physically strong, chosen for the ability to hurl their bombs a considerable distance.

A century later, grenadier duties rarely involved grenades, which were mainly used for **siege warfare**. Yet, grenadier companies remained, and were still considered the best soldiers of a regiment.

Hand grenades and rifle-launched grenades became valuable antipersonnel weapons for infantrymen in the 20th century, when much combat was against dug-in enemy soldiers or concealed machine gun positions. The American "pineapple" hand grenade gets its name from its appearance: the outside is grooved into fragments, resembling a pineapple.

This grenade is armed by pulling free a pin that governs the long, spring-loaded trigger on the outside. Held down by the soldier's hand until thrown, the trigger then springs out, and a five-second fuse is activated, followed by the explosion. ■

THROWING A GRENADE A German soldier fighting in Russia in 1941 readies to hurl a stick grenade, nicknamed a "potato masher," at an enemy position.

G

Guerrilla Warfare

Guerilla troops fight in small-scale irregular forces that conduct limited actions against an established "conventional" military, then quickly withdraw to a safe area. There, they hide and reorganize to strike again by surprise.

The term "guerrilla" means those who carry out a "small war," and comes from the Spanish *guerra*, war. Guerrillas usually have a political strategy, aiming to damage or intimidate an established government in order to shake its foundations, eventually to bring it down or change its policies. Guerrillas usually live as fugitives, often in physical hardship, so they must be totally committed to their cause. Terror is usually a key weapon, especially for urban guerrillas, who operate in populated areas. Guerrilla tactics strike at an enemy's weak points, avoiding his strengths.

Guerrilla warfare requires support from part of the local population. Aid from civilians, whether willing or compulsory, is an essential element for the success of guerrilla warfare. In the 20th century, Viet Cong guerrilla forces hid in the jungles of Vietnam or mingled with the civilian population until a preplanned moment came to strike. The Viet Cong were successful in bringing down the government of South Vietnam, but many guerrilla wars last for generations without conclusion.

Long-term guerrilla conflict causes great suffering and economic hardship. The population is constantly fearful, menaced by the threat of violence from both guerrillas and the conventional forces hunting for them. ■

Gunpowder

Also known as black powder, gunpowder was the first detonating and propellant explosive. In China, it was used for fireworks as early as the 10th century, although not yet in firearms.

Black powder is a mixture of saltpeter (potassium nitrate), sulfur, and charcoal. Its formula may have been known to so-called magicians long before the Christian era. When ignited, black powder burns rapidly and creates a gas that can propel missiles from an enclosed cylinder—such as the barrel of a gun.

Several countries, including England, Germany, and Italy, claim to have been the first to use black powder charges and firearms, but historians are uncertain about the facts. In 1304, Arabs used a bamboo and iron gun that fired arrows. Over the centuries, European gunnery improved upon black powder charges, carefully measuring them in proportion to the type and size of the cannon and the projectile being fired.

In the 17th century, black powder began to be used to blast rock for mining, road-building, and tunneling. Black powder is classified as a "low explosive" compared to more powerful chemical explosives. The "high explosives" nitroglycerin and nitrocellulose supplanted black powder for blasting purposes in the mid-19th century. ■

IN A SHELTERING HIDEOUT A Viet Cong guerrilla soldier of the Vietnam War crouches in an earthen bunker with his rifle at the ready.

GUNPOWDER FLASK

Soldier and hunter alike had to keep their precious powder dry, for they could not fire their guns with damp gunpowder. Even the slightest moisture made gunpowder useless, and it had to be thrown away. This elaborate 19th-century brass gunpowder bottle was watertight, protecting the black powder inside. The cap when reversed makes a convenient funnel, and there is a spring loaded shutter that allows just the right amount of powder to be poured. This civilian flask was probably used for fine priming powder, which was poured onto the flintlock's priming pan.

H

Hadrian's Wall

Roman emperor Hadrian ordered the construction of a frontier wall in Britain to defend against invasions and raids by the warlike Celtic tribes in the North.

Built over more than a decade and completed in the year 136, Hadrian's Wall stretched across the northern reaches of the Roman Empire in Britain. It was more than 73 miles long, from Wallsend on the River Tyne to Bowness on the Solway Firth. The wall was of turf and stone, six feet high and eight feet across, with fortifications (called Mile Castles) strategically placed along the way.

Attackers twice broke through Hadrian's Wall, in 197 and 296, but it was restored each time. When a third breakthrough destroyed much of the wall in 367–368, it was abandoned as a defensive works. Its remains are among the largest Roman constructions still to be seen in Great Britain. ■

Half-track

In the years between World Wars I and II, military thinking moved toward the "mechanization" of infantry. This meant providing foot soldiers with vehicles, wheeled and tracked, to maneuver swiftly into battle. "Motorized" infantry were loaded on trucks, armored cars, and halftracks.

Halftracks are equipped with wheels in front and tractor tracks in the rear. Sometimes designated as a "personnel carrier," the halftrack is armored to protect its troops, and might be armed with an **anti-aircraft gun** or a machine gun to support ground forces. ■

Hannibal (247–182BC)

Hannibal led the armies of Carthage against Rome in the Second **Punic War** (218–201BC). Born in North Africa, he was the son of Hamilcar, a great Carthaginian general. For many decades, Rome and

MEMORY OF ROMAN POWER
Hadrian's Wall crosses through windswept Northumberland, England; sections of the wall have been restored, other parts look much as they did in the 3rd century.

Carthage were bitter rivals for supremacy in the Mediterranean.

Rome's military was far mightier, but Hannibal proved himself superior to any Roman general of his time. Although usually outnumbered by the Romans, whose infantry, "legionnaires," were considered the best soldiers of the day, Hannibal dealt Rome some of the greatest defeats of its history.

Hannibal took command of the Carthaginian army in 221BC, at the age of 26. His early victories weakened Rome's grip on Spain, and next he led his army across the Pyrenees and the Alps and into northern Italy. His great victory at Lake Trasimene in 217BC wiped out a **Roman army** of more than 40,000 legionnaires. At Cannae in 216BC, Hannibal defeated a second Roman army, this one numbering 85,000. His force was half that of Rome's, but his skillful maneuvering and brilliant use of cavalry brought him victory, while Rome lost 50,000 men.

Hannibal campaigned for many years through Italy, but the Roman army was too large, and it prevented a direct attack on the city of Rome. When his homeland of Carthage came under Roman assault in 203BC, Hannibal hurried back, meeting defeat in North Africa. Peace was made between Rome and Carthage, but Hannibal remained an enemy of Rome for the rest of his life. He took part in military confrontations with Rome in other parts of the empire, but without success.

Threatened with capture in Syria around 184BC, Hannibal committed suicide at the age of 64. ■

Harrier Jet

The British-built Harrier Jet was the first fixed-wing combat aircraft capable of vertical takeoffs and landings (VTOL). The Harrier's VTOL capabilities make it the ideal combat aircraft in situations where adequate air fields or **aircraft carriers** are not available.

The Harrier has engine nozzles that can be rotated, enabling the aircraft to hover on the jet blast. This capability is termed "vectored thrust." The Harrier is not a supersonic fighter, and is relatively slow, but outstanding maneuverability offered by the rotating engine nozzles gives it an advantage in low-level dogfights.

The Sea Harrier, a version of the Harrier jet, can take off from a ship's deck without the need for a runway. ■

Heavy Artillery

Employed for the defense of fortifications and seaports and as siege guns, heavy artillery was not mobile until the 19th century.

Siege guns of the 15th-century were the first heavy artillery, and were essential for breaching fortified walls and knocking down heavy gates. Early siege guns fired cannonballs of 200 pounds a range of several hundred yards. The higher-velocity heavy guns of the 18th century fired smaller cannonballs, often of 24 lbs., but with tremendous impact and great accuracy. "Big guns" fired larger projectiles, sending them farther than smaller field guns could. Field guns were mainly for action against troops on the battlefield.

As defensive guns, heavy artillery required permanent emplacements protected by masonry fortifications. These installations

MARINE CORPS HARRIER
An AV-8B Harrier with a Marine expeditionary unit streaks down a ship's runway, taking off for a mission over Afghanistan in support of Operation Enduring Freedom, 2001.

HORSE

From ancient times until the 19th century, fighters on horseback were the shock troops whose gallant charge could scatter infantry, and whose patrols were the eyes of an army.

Cavalry might be Scythian bowmen or mounted squadrons of heavily armed Athenian hoplites. Cavalry includes medieval **knights** in armor on thundering war horses, as well as Polish lancers and their enemies, the fast-riding Russian Cossacks. Among the world's finest light cavalry were the Indians of the Great American West, who fought another excellent cavalry force—blue-coated U.S. army troopers.

The horse was a draft animal in ancient times, making its first military appearance pulling battle **chariots** in the 15th century BC. Mounted warriors came to the fore around 900BC, and the horse became important to most armies of the civilized world. By the 15th century, the horse was hauling cannons into battle. In the 19th century, horse-drawn field guns became a key to victory, as daring horse-artillery batteries determined the outcome of many major battles.

The horse was less important after the 19th century, and by the end of **World War II** (1939–45) cavalry was obsolete. In modern armies, the horse was replaced by the motorized vehicle and by **helicopters**. Yet, horses sometimes carried soldiers into action. In 2001, American Special Forces in Afghanistan rode horseback through country too rugged and remote for motorized vehicles.

Swift-riding Plains Indian warriors were among the best light cavalry of the 19th century.

An 1880s cavalryman in full dress shows off Comanche, the only survivor of the Seventh Cavalry massacre by Plains Indians at the Battle of Little Big Horn.

A fierce Japanese rider wields a pole arm in battle near Kagoshima, on Japan's Kyushu Island.

Arab horsemen of North Africa and the Middle East breed horses that are prized around the world.

French artillerymen bring up field guns in fighting on the Somme River in World War I.

H

HOWITZER

Developed in the 18th century, howitzers are cannons that have shorter barrels and are designed to fire low-velocity shells over defensive obstacles. A medium-range artillery piece, the howitzer sends shells in a high trajectory, so that they fall upon enemy positions rather than striking from straight ahead. Eighteenth century howitzers could also fire canisters—bullet-sized antipersonnel projectiles that scatter after leaving the gun barrel. During the Russo-Japanese War (1904–05), the Japanese howitzers that bombarded Port Arthur with 550-lb. shells were the heaviest land guns ever used until that time. Later howitzers of the 20th century were effective field artillery that could be quickly moved into position by or on motorized vehicles. In fact, most modern field guns are howitzers.

Korean War 155mm self-propelled howitzer

called for a large number of crewmen to serve the guns. They also required a reliable source of ammunition which, itself, needed secure magazines for storage.

By the mid-19th century, heavy guns fired hollow shells loaded with explosives and fitted with a fuse timed to detonate when they reached their targets. The heaviest guns had a range of several miles. Late in the century, the largest artillery pieces were transported on **railroad** carriages hauled by locomotives. In **World War I** (1914–18), a German "railway gun" cannonaded Paris from 60 miles away, firing shells weighing 264 lbs. This gun's maximum range was 82 miles.

After **World War II** (1939–45) heavy artillery pieces were motorized and were designed to fire shells—some with nuclear warheads—more than 5,000 yards. ∎

HELICOPTER DRILL Members of an Explosive Ordnance Disposal unit "fast rope" from a helicopter onto the flight deck of the USS *Enterprise* during a training exercise.

Helicopter

This aircraft acquires lift and thrust from the turning of its rotors. Modern armies rely on helicopters for battlefield support of troops on the ground and to carry soldiers into action over almost any kind of terrain.

The first military helicopters came into use in the late 1940s and early 1950s, mainly for for reconnaissance, for transporting light cargo, and for evacuating wounded. By the 1960s, helicopters had more powerful engines that gave greater speed and performance. In this time, the French began to arm military helicopters to combat the Algerian uprising, and attack helicopters—armored, and carrying heavy machine guns and rockets—were employed by Americans and South Vietnamese in the **Vietnam War**.

In Vietnam, attack helicopters, such as the Apache, carried cannons, 70mm rockets, and guided missiles capable of striking a target a mile away. Large twin-engine Chinook helicopters could carry up to 35,000 pounds of supplies and heavy equipment, while formations of smaller and faster Black Hawk helicopters transported **airborne troopers**—known as air cavalry. Small Kiowa scout "choppers," as helicopters are nicknamed, were equipped with television cameras and infrared "eyes" for observation.

Although vulnerable to rocket fire from the ground, the helicopter is among the most indispensable weapons of any modern army. ∎

Horse Artillery

French and Prussian gunners of the 18th century were among the first to ride horses when maneuvering their artillery pieces into battlefield position. Other artillery crews marched on foot alongside their guns.

Horse artillery reached its zenith in the French armies of the **Napoleonic Wars** (1802–15). **Napoleon Bonaparte,** himself an

artillerist, trained his horse artillery to race into battlefield positions. These elite mounted crews galloped alongside their **field cannons,** which were pulled into action by a team of horses. When their assigned position was reached, the crews dismounted, swiftly unlimbered the cannons, and went into action. By the early 20th century, most field artillery was organized as horse artillery.

In **World War I** (1914–18) motorized vehicles began to replace horses for hauling field guns. **World War II** (1939–45) saw the development of self-propelled artillery pieces that were driven into battle. ■

Hundred Years' War

In 1337, King Edward III of England commanded his armies to devastate northwestern France in order to force the French king, Philip VI, to submit to his demands. Edward claimed to be the rightful ruler of France. Further, he objected to the French alliance with Scotland, a nation that was hostile to him.

Edward's marauding started a conflict with France that lasted more than 115 years, and was called The Hundred Years War. The English won the most important battles—Crécy (1346), Poitiers (1356), and Agincourt (1415)—but these victories achieved no decisive result. Other kingdoms also were drawn in: England made alliances with Portugal and Burgundy, and France allied with Castile. The inspired leadership of Joan of Arc, especially at the siege of Orleans (1428), helped the French win final victory. The war ended as a French triumph in 1453, when almost all the English troops were driven from the continent. ■

Hydrogen Bomb

Also known as a thermonuclear weapon, this bomb creates an explosion equal to thousands of tons of TNT. The hydrogen bomb's power derives from the process of atomic fission.

"Thermonuclear" refers to the heat energy released by the process of nuclear fission and also to the chemicals that cause the explosion. The explosion results from radiation bombarding uranium, which releases electromagnetic radiation that "sparks" a chemical compound of lithium and heavy hydrogen. This process creates a high-temperature fireball.

This radiation causes severe illness among those people who are exposed to it. "Fallout" from the debris that the explosion hurls high into the atmosphere is "radioactive"—contaminated with this radiation and dangerous to all living things. ■

AN ENGLISH VICTORY
While the lilies of France and English lions float above the 1356 Battle of Poitiers, English long-bowmen look on as foot soldiers clash with battle axes and spears.

I

ICBM—Intercontinental Ballistic Missile

These are land-based, guided missiles with a range of more than 3,300 miles.

"Ballistic" missiles are "thrown," propelled by a rocket that burns out after sending the warheads on a trajectory. **Cruise missiles,** on the other hand, fly through the atmosphere. The ICBM is guided by internal systems that keep it on course as it travels at more than 16,000-mph. The missile can rise hundreds of miles into space on its trajectory, then reenter the atmosphere.

ICBMs are fired from both permanent sites and mobile launchers. Permanent ICBM sites include in-ground silos that are fortified and concealed from observation.

Mobile launchers can be **railroad** cars or motorized vehicles.

ICBMs are armed with conventional or nuclear warheads—usually with several warheads on each missile. ■

India-Pakistan Wars

Pakistan, which is mostly Muslim, and India, which is mostly Hindu, have been hostile to each other since the Indian subcontinent became independent in 1947. During the early years of independence, there was bloody rioting between Hindus and Muslims, leaving a lasting antagonism between both peoples.

The first major war between India and Pakistan occurred in 1965, as Pakistan claimed authority over Indian-controlled Kashmir, which is largely Muslim. Ground offensives and counteroffensives, combined with air strikes, ended in stalemate. Pakistani armor suffered heavy losses, and so did India's air force, which was attacked while still on the ground.

The second India-Pakistan war was in 1971. The conflict was sparked by the East Pakistan independence movement, which was being forcibly repressed by the Pakistani government, but was supported by India.

Once again, the Pakistani air force launched a preemptive strike, but India was prepared and won overwhelming air superiority over the eastern battlefront. Indian troops invaded East Pakistan and allied themselves with an army of 100,000 insurgents fighting for independence. These allies captured more than 90,000 Pakistani troops in a victory that laid the

ICBM TEST-FIRING
A Minuteman III intercontinental ballistic missile blasts off with smoke and a roar from a pad at Vandenberg Air Force Base on the coast of California in 1982.

foundation for the independence of East Pakistan, which became Bangladesh. ∎

Indian Wars in the American West

After the American Revolution (1775–83), native peoples fought a century-long struggle with the westward-migrating settlers, who were backed by government troops. Known as the Indian Wars, these conflicts are grouped into two major periods: 1789–1865 and 1865–91.

Native fighters were successful against the first armies sent into their territory until General Anthony Wayne defeated the Ohio-region tribes at Fallen Timbers in 1794. The government won victories over the powerful Shawnees at Tippecanoe in 1811 and then later against the Creeks, Cherokees, and Seminoles of the South. These nations were forced to migrate westward to permanent reservations. In 1862, a Sioux uprising against settlers in the Midwest brought harsh reprisals against the rebellious warriors and their chiefs.

DEATH OF A WAR CHIEF Fifty frontier scouts were surrounded by hundreds of Sioux and Cheyenne at Beecher's Island, Colorado, in 1868; the assaults were beaten off, this one costing the life of Cheyenne leader Roman Nose.

After 1865, the Indian wars involved the western nations of the Great Plains and the Apaches of the Southwest. Illegal settlement, gold rushes, and corruption in the reservation system brought the Indians into frequent conflict with whites. Clashes resulted in army campaigns that destroyed villages and forced more nations onto reservations.

In 1876, a force of mainly Sioux and Cheyenne, led by Sitting Bull and Crazy Horse, wiped out General George A. Custer's expedition at the Little Big Horn River in Montana. Their triumph was short-lived, however, as the military finally forced them onto reservations. Among the last hostiles were Southwest Apache renegades led by Geronimo, who surrendered in 1886. The last so-called battle of the Indian Wars was the army's massacre of a captive Sioux band at Wounded Knee, South Dakota, in 1890.

There were 1,065 Indian Wars engagements between 1866 and 1891. Army casualties were 932 killed and 1,061 wounded, but no firm estimates of Indian losses are available. Fighting peaked in 1867–69, including 140 engagements in 1868. ∎

Indochina-France War

After **World War II** (1939–45), France attempted to recover her colonies in Indochina. These colonies included Laos, Cambodia, and Vietnam. Throughout the war, Japanese occupation of the region had been resisted by nationalist guerrillas, who were determined to prevent the French from reestablishing a colonial regime.

Led by the Communist Ho Chi Minh (Nguyen That Thanh), insurgents known as Viet Minh (Vietnam Independence League), were supported by Communist China. The French and their Vietnamese loyalists were aided by the United States. The French controlled the major cities, but the Viet Minh moved freely in the country.

In 1953, the French established a central military base at Dien Bien Phu, but it

I INFANTRY

The Roman legionary of the 1st century AD was the finest infantryman of his time.

Soldiers who fight on foot, the infantry is the largest part of any army. The foot soldier guards against invasion by enemy infantry and is the one who first enters the opposition's territory. Infantry take and hold cities and military positions and establish control over the enemy population.

Armed with swords, spears, **shields,** and bows, early foot soldiers wore various types of armor. The Greek infantry fought in solid, unyielding **phalanxes,** which the Romans later transformed into highly mobile **legions** composed of several detachable units.

By the 17th century the infantry had no armor but carried guns and bayonets and fought in extended firing lines. Dramatic improvements in firearms and artillery in the 20th century changed infantry tactics accordingly. Foot soldiers began to operate in smaller, more independent units that communicated by radios and telephones. Modern infantry, equipped with automatic rifles and rocket launchers, can be transported into action by motorized vehicles and **helicopters,** or dropped by parachute.

No matter how they fought, the infantry's basic task has remained the same throughout the ages: take a position and hold it.

The American 442 Regimental Combat Team fought across Italy and France; made up of Japanese and Hawaiian Americans, the 442 was the most decorated unit in the World War II army.

An American G.I. carries everything he needs—goggles, body armor, a light machine gun, bedroll, and his full backpack.

A Revolutionary War officer shouts an order to infantrymen in his command.

was soon besieged by the Viet Minh, who captured it the following year. Unwilling to wage a full-scale, costly war for Indochina, France abandoned the region, leaving Vietnam divided into a communist North and an anti-communist South. The subsequent struggle between these two regions eventually drew in the United States in support of South Vietnam. ∎

Iran-Iraq War

Also known as the First Persian Gulf War, this was the world's greatest conflict—in terms of duration and the number of casualties—since **World War II**. Iraq had a far better armed and equipped army, but Iranian fanaticism resisted its attacks, and neither side could win the struggle. Iran had more men, but Iraq had the backing of the United States and other Arab countries.

Fighting started in 1980 and stopped several times, with neither side able to gain a decisive advantage. The war became a standoff, and peace was negotiated in 1988. ∎

Ironclad Warships

First developed in the United States and Europe in the mid-19th century, these vessels were the forerunners of the **battleships** that appeared a few years later. Artillery barges armored with iron had been employed by the British and French in the **Crimean War** (1853–56), but the first true, iron-plated warship was France's *Gloire*. Built in 1859, she had plates, four and a half inches, thick fastened to a heavy timber hull. *Gloire* was powered by both steam and sail.

Early in the American Civil War (1861–65), ironclad steam-powered gunboats were used by the Union forces on the Mississippi. The most famous ironclad warships of the day were the Union *Monitor* and the Confederate *Virginia* (formerly named *Merrimack*).

In March 1862, these ironclads dueled inconclusively at Hampton Roads, Virginia. The world took note of their formidable design and of how, in the days before the engagement, *Virginia* had wreaked havoc with the wooden warships of the Union fleet.

Stimulated by the success of the *Monitor* and *Virginia*, the world's great naval powers began to produce ever larger and faster ironclad warships.

By 1890, several nations possessed iron-hulled **battleships**–also known as "capital ships"–the most powerful warships in the world. ∎

FIRST PERSIAN GULF WAR
Iranian soldiers are parading near their positions at the front line during the Iran-Iraq War of 1980–88. This bloody conflict began with an Iraqi invasion of western Iran in an attempt to capture a key waterway. The Iraqis made early gains, but after a few years the Iranians drove them out and forced peace terms to be accepted. It is estimated that 1.5 million Iraqis and Iranians died in almost nine years of war.

IRONCLADS CLASH The Confederate ironclad ram, *Virginia*—formerly the *Merrimack*—fights the new Union ironclad gunboat *Monitor* to a draw at Hampton Roads, Virginia, in 1862.

J-K

Jacobite Rebellions

The Jacobites supported the exiled king, James II, and his Stuart descendants, who claimed the British throne. (*Jacobus* is Latin for James.) The Jacobite movement thrived in the decades between the 1688 "Glorious Revolution" in England and the 1745 defeat of Jacobite Prince Charles Edward Stuart at Culloden, Scotland.

In this time, with the Stuart court living in France, the Jacobite movement was strongest in Scotland, Wales, and Ireland. Jacobite rebellions in 1715 and 1745 were put down by the British government. At Culloden Moor in 1745, a Jacobite army of Scottish Highlanders supporting Charles Stuart, "Bonnie Prince Charlie," met the army of King George II, which was pursuing them. The Highlanders charged recklessly against the waiting royal army and were slaughtered.

Prince Charles narrowly escaped and returned to France, ending the final chance for the Stuart restoration. ■

"THE 'FORTY-FIVE' INSURRECTION
Scottish Jacobites won the first battles in their 1745 rebellion against King George II, including the defeat of a government force at the battle of Prestonpans in September.

Jet Aircraft

Toward the end of **World War II** (1939–45), Britain and Germany developed fighter planes driven by jet propulsion, which is forward thrust that is powered by rearward discharge of a jet of fluid. This jet is a mixture of air with the gas that results from the combustion of fuel.

The jet was developed too late to be a decisive factor in World War II, but its greater speed and ability to fly higher than piston-engine combat planes opened an astonishing new world of aeronautics. Just two years after the war, test pilots in jets were flying faster than the speed of sound. Jet airplanes took on the characteristic swept-back wing design that made such high speeds possible.

Jet fighters first were used in the **Korean War** (1950–53), and before long almost all fixed-wing combat aircraft–fighters, bombers, and transport aircraft–had jet engines.

Historians consider the invention of jet-propelled warplanes to be the most significant military result of World War II. ■

King George's War

Part of a greater conflict known as the **War of the Austrian Succession** (1740–48), this was a struggle between French and British

colonies in North America. It was named after the reigning British king, George II.

War began in Europe between the great powers, and the news reached the French colonies before the British. This gave the French the advantage of surprise, which they used for some early victories. The New England colonists called upon Parliament to capture the newly built French fortress of Louisburg on Cape Breton. Parliament refused, saying such a campaign would be too costly and too difficult. New England and New York militias then sent their own expedition against Louisburg, capturing it in June 1745.

The Louisburg triumph was a point of great pride to the colonists, but the war was largely a series of brutal border raids and counter-raids. To the dismay of the colonists, the peace treaty in 1748 gave Louisburg back to the French in exchange for other possessions. The embittered

AMBUSHED A 19th-century depiction of the death of King Philip, ambushed in a swamp by New England militia and native allies.

Americans never forgave Parliament for what they thought was a betrayal of their dearly won victory.

These hard feelings, especially among New Englanders, played a large part in the events leading up to the American Revolution in 1775. ■

King Philip's War

As the New England colonies expanded and increased in population, the native peoples felt they were being forced out of the region. These tribes included the Wampanoag, Narragansett, Nipmuc, Abenaki, and others in the Connecticut and Hudson river valleys.

Indeed, the Indians were declining in numbers and were suffering from disease. Also, they were losing their former influence with the colonists, whom they had helped get established a few decades earlier. At the same time, the colonists were prospering, becoming ever more numerous, with a flow of newcomers from England also eager for land.

At the forefront of native resistance was the Wampanoag sachem (chief), who was named "King Philip" by the settlers, Metacomet by his own people. He formed an alliance of the tribes to oppose expansion by the colonists.

In June 1675, when colonists executed three Wampanoags for the murder of another Indian, the tribes rose up in anger. They attacked settlements and travelers, winning an early advantage over the colonists and destroying many frontier communities. The coming of winter, however, quickly brought hardships to the native villages. At the same time, the colonists enlisted Christianized—"praying"—Indians to help fight the hostile tribes. The better-armed colonists launched devastating attacks that destroyed several villages.

By August 1676, Philip had been killed, weakening his people's ability to fight on. Peace soon was made, but more than 600

PIPE TOMAHAWK
Smoking tobacco was an important ceremony to American native peoples, who prized European-made trade tomahawks that were also designed as pipes. The tomahawk head has a bowl for burning tobacco, and the handle is hollow. Pipe tomahawks were especially made for traders to carry into the wilderness and offer to the tribes in exchange for furs. By the 18th century, most native peoples in America depended on the manufactured goods, including firearms and ammunition, that were bought from white traders.

K

Medieval
dagger, its
wooden grip
covered in
leather and wire.

Wooden shield,
decorated with
fleur-de-lis.

German 15th-century
"armet" helmet, one
of the most effective
of all medieval
helmet types.

whites had lost their lives, and many Indian villages had been wiped out, the survivors forced to flee. Much of New England now was open to further settlement by the colonists. ■

Knight

The term comes from an Old English word for mounted warrior.

The knight was the most prominent individual in Europe during the late Middle Ages (700–1400). This was the age of the feudal system, when the lord ruled vassals, who swore him allegiance. The lord granted the knight an estate, known as a fief, in return for military service. In times of war or when a **castle** guard was needed, the knight served at the will of his lord. The knight, in turn, had his own vassals who gave him their allegiance.

As a mounted fighting man, the knight became ever more heavily armored, as did his horse, called a charger. At first, knights were formidable figures on the battlefield, and wars often hung on their combat. Eventually, powerful archery and the foot soldier's long-handled pole arms and spears made the mounted knight less important in battle. The English victories of the **Hundred Years' War** cost the lives of thousands of French knights whose chargers became mired in mud. Hampered by their heavy armor and unable to get their horses free, these knights were killed by hails of English arrows and by swarming foot soldiers, who overpowered them.

As **mercenary** (professional) soldiers

KNIGHTS IN ARMOR The glory of the medieval knight was to vanquish a foe in single combat with lances and on horseback, as depicted here by a 15th-century French artist.

came into general use in the 14th century, knights often substituted a money payment to their lords instead of embarking on military service. Many knights refused to accept their feudal military responsibilities, which included the cost of a suit of armor, chargers, weapons, and attendants.

In response to the need for loyal knights, kings began to create them in mass ceremonies that demanded the new knight's oath of allegiance to the throne. ■

Korean War

The first war fought by the United Nations, this conflict was brought on when the communist Democratic People's Republic of North Korea launched a surprise attack on the non-communist Republic of South Korea.

After **World War II,** Japanese forces in the northern part of the Korean peninsula surrendered to the Soviet Union, and those in the South to the U.S. The 38th parallel became a political boundary between the communist-ruled North and the republic in the South. North Korea, however, claimed authority over all the peninsula.

Armed by China and the Soviet Union, North Korea attacked with 127,000 troops in June 1950. They drove the unprepared South Koreans and their 500 American advisors all the way to the southern coast. A force to oppose the North Koreans was prepared immediately under the authority of the UN.

In September, American general Douglas MacArthur made an amphibious landing with U.S. forces at Inchon, near the South Korean capital of Seoul. Commander-in-chief MacArthur cut off and captured 125,000 North Korean invaders. Ignoring threats by China, he drove up the peninsula, and by November was near the Chinese border.

China then sent thousands of "volunteers" into Korea. They pushed back MacArthur's troops, who included the soldiers of a dozen UN-member nations.

MacArthur soon regrouped and resumed the offensive. He wanted to strike at China, but was forbidden by President Harry S. Truman because of political considerations. The aggressive MacArthur was removed from command in April 1951.

The war had dragged to a stalemate by then, but truce talks made no progress for many more months. Armistice terms finally established the 38th parallel as the boundary between North and South Korea. This became the most heavily armed border in the world.

The Korean War cost the lives of five million civilians and soldiers. UN forces lost 447,697 dead and 547,904 wounded and missing; of this number, the U.S. had 29,550 dead and 106,978 wounded, South Korea 415,004 dead and 428,568 wounded or missing. North Korean casualties have been estimated at 520,000, and Chinese casualties at 900,000. ■

BLEAK WAR ZONE
American G.I.s slog through cold and barren Korea, where harsh winter conditions caused many casualties and much sickness during the Korean War.

Laser-guided "Smart" Bombs

This weaponry is controlled by built-in electronic technology that directs the bomb at the target.

Remote-controlled "smart" bombs are capable of altering course in order to strike home. They are steered by reflected infrared radiation that is bounced off the target by a ground observer or an aircraft.

The smart bomb's laser-guidance system locks onto the beam and aims for the target. These weapons are credited with limiting civilian casualties and unnecessary destruction because they can be aimed so accurately.

In the **Vietnam War** (1960–75), early radio-guided smart missiles were fired from combat aircraft and directed by the pilot, who steered them, by eye, with a control stick. Later, a television camera on the aircraft aided the pilot to control these weapons. Laser guidance came next, as bombs were fitted with sensors that sought out a point lit by a laser beam that is bounced off the target. Infrared imaging devices further improved accuracy by detecting the infrared light that is emitted from a target.

In the 1990–91 **Persian Gulf War,** smart weapons, with laser and optical guidance systems, struck their targets an estimated 75 per cent of the time. ■

Lee, Robert E. (1807–70)

One of America's most respected military leaders, Lee commanded the Confederate armies in the Civil War (1861–65). A former superintendent of the U.S. military academy at West Point, Lee had served in the **Mexican War** (1846–48) and was a career army officer at the time of Southern secession from the Union. He at first opposed secession.

Lee was offered overall command of Union forces, but his loyalty to his home state of Virginia compelled him to turn down the offer. He resigned from the army and returned to Virginia, which left the Union in April 1861.

At the start of hostilities, Lee served as a military advisor to the Confederacy, and in 1862 assumed command of the Army of Northern Virginia. He became commander-in-chief of all Confederate forces while continuing to lead an army in the field. Lee orchestrated major victories at the Seven Days' battles (1862), Fredericksburg (1862), and Chancellorsville (1863). His defeat at the battle of Gettysburg in mid-1863

LEE MEETS JACKSON
Confederate commander Robert E. Lee, right, meets Thomas "Stonewall" Jackson, one of his top generals, during a campaign in Northern Virginia. Lee is on his favorite horse, "Traveler." The troops behind Jackson are on the march, with the battle flag of the Confederate States of America flying above them.

marked the beginning of the end of the Confederacy. After almost two more years of defensive warfare against **Ulysses S. Grant's** vastly larger Union army, Lee surrendered at Appomattox Court House, Virginia, on April 9, 1865. This effectively ended the Civil War. ■

Legion

This Roman military unit replaced the once-dominant Macedonian **phalanx** made famous by **Alexander the Great**. The slow-moving phalanx, with thousands of tightly packed pikemen carrying long, heavy pikes was not as flexible in action as the Roman legion.

The legion formation, which came to the fore in the 4th century BC, had 4-6,000 infantry divided into tactical units of 60-100 men, called centuries. In battle formation, each century cooperated with another century in a unit called a maniple. The entire legion formed a line of battle three maniples deep. Space between each maniple permitted the advance of maniples from the rear or the withdrawal of maniples in the front line. From the 1st century BC onward, the legion was divided into cohorts, each with 10 centuries. These smaller units gave the legion its flexibility in battle.

The Roman legionary used a short stabbing sword and carried a large, rectangular **shield** for close fighting, unlike phalanx pikemen, whose small shields hung from their necks so they had both hands to hold the pike. The Roman infantry fought under the pikes to stab and slash at the pikemen, who were not well equipped for such close action. ■

Longbow, English

The six-foot-tall bow made of English yew was the best missile weapon of war from the 14th to the 16th centuries.

The longbow required tall and strong archers, for it took as much as 100 lbs. of force to draw back the hempen bowstring. The archer used his first two fingers to draw the 37-inch arrow, which was fletched with goose feathers. Able to pierce armor, the longbow had an effective range of 200 yards.

During the great battles of the **Hundred Years' War** (1337–1453), English archers slaughtered thousands of French armored **knights**. If an English archer was captured by the French, his two string fingers were often amputated, and he was sent back to his own army, useless as an archer. This was intended as a serious insult to the English. Before battles, or whenever English archers were confronting French soldiers, a favorite counter-insult was for the archers to hold up their first two fingers, warning the French that they could still fire their longbows. ■

TAKING AIM
An English archer from the 14th-century reign of Edward III raises his longbow as massed archers in the distance prepare to fire; Edward's reputation as a master military leader in the Hundred Years' War was earned, in part, by the skill of his archers.

73

M

Mail

Also called "chain mail," this armor was a metal fabric of small iron links or rings joined together. Probably invented by the Celts as early as the 5th century BC, mail was fashioned to cover the head, limbs, and hands. Each ring commonly had four others attached to it, making it a fabric that could be shaped for the part of the body it covered.

A hauberk was a long shirt of mail that reached below the knees and covered the arms to the elbows. The sleeves sometimes extended to protect the wearer's hands. The hauberk was worn over a close-fitting quilted undershirt for comfort. When **plate armor** was worn, mail protected knee joints, neck, and elbows, which had to be flexible.

Mail was common battlefield gear until the 16th century, when firearms began to change warfare. As edged weapons were replaced by firearms, mail fell out of use in western Europe. It was still worn in parts of Asia until the 17th century, and even as late as the 1900s mail shirts were used in the Caucuses of southern Russia. ■

M16-A1 Rifle

A shoulder-fired weapon, the M16-A1 and its later designs were improvements on the M16 assault rifle that first served American forces in the **Vietnam War** (1960–75).

The M16-A1 assault rifle was favored by many armies and guerrilla forces around the world at the end of the 20th century. The first assault rifles were designed during **World War II** (1939–45) to give the infantryman a high rate of fire. The M16-A1 was manufactured by the Colt Company, which in 1959 acquired the production rights from Armalite, the inventor. Armalite's name for its first model of this rifle was AR15, which in 1967 was renamed by Colt as the M16. The weapon was subsequently improved in the next model, M16-A1.

Gas-operated and air-cooled, the M16-A1 has a magazine of 20 rounds and can be set on automatic or semi-automatic. On automatic setting, it can fire 700-800 rounds per minute with an effective range—distance in which the bullet can cause casualties—of approximately 500 yards. The next rifle model, with improvements in accuracy and in firing control, was the M16-A2. ■

FIRING FROM COVER
Lying prone behind the shelter of a log, an American soldier trains with an M16-A2 assault rifle; for rifle training, the soldier wears camouflage fatigues rather than full combat gear.

MACHINE GUN

The machine gun fires large quantities of ammunition from a magazine or a belt, without the need for frequent reloading. The first primitive machine gun was proposed in England in 1718, but it was not to be developed as a weapon until the 19th century.

Most early machine guns used a hand-crank to bring the fresh cartridge into position and at the same time eject the spent shell casing. Several models tried in the American Civil War (1861–65) had little success because the machine gun crews lacked experience, and the ammunition sometimes jammed or did not fire properly.

Improved machine guns and ammunition were developed later in the century, and in **World War I** (1914–18) the weapon's devastating firepower was finally proven. Frontal attacks by infantry were doomed wherever they met massed machine guns, which were used by the thousands on every battle front.

The machine gun became war's dominant firearm, fitted on aircraft, tanks, and warships and used on almost every modern combat vehicle. The most powerful of all machine guns are Gatling-style and can fire thousands of rounds a minute. The heavy, .50-caliber Gatling-style machine guns on **helicopter** gunships can offer overwhelmingly destructive fire-support to troops on the ground.

A Gatling gun on exhibit in Winston, North Carolina, in the early 1900s.

A World War I American machine gun crew under fire in France.

Ammunition belt

Water jacket

World War II era water-cooled machine gun, with a can of water feeding the jacket that encases the barrel.

Tripod

Water reservoir

Ammunition can

U.S. Marines train with an M-240G machine gun at Camp Lejune, North Carolina, in the 1990s.

MEDALS, AWARDS, HONORS

George Washington created the Badge of Military Merit—a cloth purple heart—awarded to Revolutionary War soldiers for outstanding service.

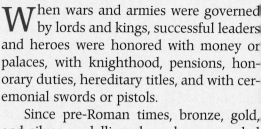

When wars and armies were governed by lords and kings, successful leaders and heroes were honored with money or palaces, with knighthood, pensions, honorary duties, hereditary titles, and with ceremonial swords or pistols.

Since pre-Roman times, bronze, gold, and silver medallions have been awarded as tokens of a leader's gratitude, or a nation's admiration. Military honors range from medals to special designations given to military units. For example, the term "royal" indicates that a British regiment—the Royal Scots Greys, or Royal Welsh Fusiliers—was especially honored by the monarch. Outstanding heroes are given membership in honorary organizations, such as the French Legion of Honor and the British Order of the Garter.

Most modern nations award servicemen and women with medals commemorating their participation in a war or in some theater of action. In certain cases of distinguished service, a soldier might be "Mentioned in Dispatches" that were sent to headquarters from a battlefield. The U.S. Purple Heart is awarded to those who are wounded in action. Medals for courage above and beyond the call of duty are the most valued of military honors. The best known of these awards include the U.S. Congressional Medal of Honor, the U.K. Victoria Cross, the German Iron Cross, and the French Croix de Guerre.

In the 1930s, the Purple Heart was designated as a medal for individuals wounded in action.

Arimoto Yamagata was a much-decorated Japanese general of the Russo-Japanese War.

The Victoria Cross is the highest award for gallantry given by British and Commonwealth forces.

World War II army lieutenant Audie Murphy won every possible U.S. medal for valor, including the Congressional Medal of Honor.

U.S. Army Chief of Staff, General Eric Shinseki, pins the Bronze Star for valor to the chest of Special Forces captain Jason Amerine, who served in Afghanistan in 2002.

M1A1 Abrams Tank

This highly mobile heavyweight was the main U.S. battle tank in the late 20th century. Powered by a 1,500hp gas-turbine engine, the 63-ton Abrams can race into battle at 45mph and has a low profile, making it more difficult to see and to hit.

This tank's armor is made of layers of "composite" material that is stronger than steel. Its engine is relatively quiet, and its exhaust emits little smoke—factors that make the Abrams more stealthy, especially at night and in fog.

A computer-controlled fire-control system uses laser technology to calculate range and set the aim. Electronic viewing systems let the crew penetrate darkness to locate the target. Thermal Imaging Systems indicate the presence of warmth, whether from a person or the engine of a concealed enemy vehicle. Up to 5,000 yards, the Abrams can fire with 90 percent accuracy.

At the start of the 21st century, the M1A1 Abrams was considered the world's greatest fighting machine on land. ■

Maginot Line

An almost impregnable network of fortifications was built by the French after **World War I** (1914–18) to deter Nazi Germany from attacking across the Rhine or from Lorraine.

FAST AND FORMIDABLE The world's most powerful battle tank, the U.S. M1A1 Abrams, races across a desert during maneuvers in a live-fire training exercise.

The Maginot Line was an elaborate combination of strongpoints and tunnels connected by rails. Most of the fortifications were underground, with the above-ground sections constructed of thick concrete.

The works were conceived by French minister of war André Maginot, after whom they were named. The line was finished by 1938, at immense cost, and requiring 15,000 laborers.

Although the fortifications covered the 200-mile French-German frontier, an equal distance was left unfortified along France's border with Belgium. When the Germans attacked in 1940, their **"blitzkrieg"** tactics of fast-moving, massed armor avoided the formidable Maginot Line and broke through Belgium and into France.

The Maginot fortifications were useless in the campaign, which quickly ended with the fall of France to the Nazis. ■

Marines

Marines are soldiers who are trained for service aboard vessels and as elite assault troops who operate in rapid strike forces, achieve their mission, then are replaced by conventional ground troops.

Since the 18th century, virtually all navies have had marines, who protect vessels at sea and stand guard while a ship is in port. Marines first were for defending naval vessels against enemy boarders—these are often the other navy's marines. Repelling enemy boarders became a bygone duty in the 20th century, but marines still did serve on board naval vessels and garrisoned bases and port installations. Originally trained for sea battles and to make raids against enemy ports, marines have become elite troops capable of many different duties on land. The U.S. Marine Corps, founded in 1775, is part of the U.S. Navy,

MAN-AT-ARMS The fighting man with a suit of plate armor, such as this 1450s Italian-style suit, would have been a leader with considerable wealth. The man-at-arms was a heavily armed warrior, usually in the service of a lord or knight, or he was a mercenary in the pay of a city or state. During the 14th and 15th centuries, a man-at-arms would often lead a "lance," a common military unit consisting of a man-at-arms, his page (servant), a squire, and several archers—all on horseback. The three or four foot soldiers in the lance were armed with either sword, crossbow, pike, or firearm, depending on the period.

MEDICAL TREATMENT

Recuperating Civil War wounded, with doctors, nurses, and visitors, in a Washington, D.C. military hospital.

Vietnam War soldiers and medics load wounded men into an evacuation helicopter.

An American Revolution surgeon binds a wound.

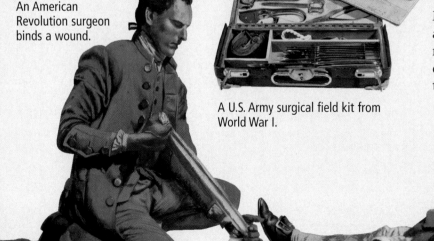

A U.S. Army surgical field kit from World War I.

Until the mid-19th century, most medical care for troops in the field was provided by camp followers—often the soldiers' families, who accompanied the army on campaign. There were few trained doctors, although armies and navies employed military "surgeons," who could treat common wounds.

For centuries, a much higher proportion of an army's losses came from illness—typhoid fever, dysentery, malaria—than from battlefield wounds. English nurse Florence Nightingale began reforming military hospitals during the **Crimean War** (1853–56). Nightingale improved hospital sanitation, reduced crowding, and provided the essential medicines and food for the soldier's recovery. Nightingale's work was an inspiration to many nations, but change was slow in coming. In the American Civil War (1861–65), for example, Union battle deaths were approximately 140,000, while more than 224,000 died from other causes.

In today's armies, medical personnel with modern methods and equipment are extremely effective, but they are often in as much danger as the soldiers they are attending. Individual "medics" serve with troops in the field and are prepared to offer first aid that keeps the casualty alive until he can be shipped to a field hospital.

Rapid evacuation is key to saving lives. Medical evacuation by **helicopter** can have a wounded soldier at a field hospital in minutes. Yet field hospitals often operate in difficult conditions, under fire and subject to bad weather and lack of supplies.

and like the navy, has its own aviation arm. Since early in the 20th century, American marines are often the first troops sent into a combat zone. ∎

Marlborough, Duke of (1650–1722)

John Churchill, 1st Duke of Marlborough, led British armies and their allies to important victories over France in the 17th and 18th centuries, and he is considered to be one of England's greatest generals.

Marlborough was successful wherever he served, from Ireland to Flanders to France. His greatest victories came in the **War of the Spanish Succession** (1701–14) against the powerful army of the French king Louis XIV. Marlborough's triumphs at Blenheim (1704), Ramillies (1706), and Oudenaarde (1708) thwarted Louis's attempt to take the Spanish throne.

Marlborough became a controversial political figure at home because he feuded with the British monarch and opposed the war-profiteers. He was more than once dismissed from command and then had it restored because he was so valuable a leader. Imprisoned for a time in the Tower of London, Marlborough even faced possible execution. When George I came to the British throne in 1714, Marlborough regained his full stature at court.

Until **Napoleon Bonaparte** rose to power in the 1790s, Marlborough was considered the greatest commander of the age. ∎

Mercenary

These are hired soldiers who fight for no other reason than to earn some payment. Mercenaries have no permanent allegiance to those who pay them.

Professional soldiers hired to fight the wars of lords and kings have existed in substantial numbers since the 13th century, when standing armies were small, or nonexistent. The mercenary was the most effective fighting man, and he was used for both offensive and defensive duties.

There was a risk in using mercenaries, however, for they might turn against their employer and fight for whomever paid them more.

After the **Hundred Years' War** (1337–1453), Europe was overrun with armed, unemployed mercenaries, who came from many nations. They were aggressive, undisciplined, brutal, treacherous, and eager for ill-gotten gain by the use of their weapons. During the 15th–18th centuries mercenaries were mostly from Germany, Switzerland, Ireland, and Italy.

In the late 20th and early 21st centuries, mercenaries still existed. Nationalist and tribal struggles in the Third World often involved mercenaries, sometimes veterans from the armies of developed countries. These soldiers profit from their training with sophisticated weapons and equipment. It can happen that both government and rebel forces hire mercenaries to handle communications and operate aircraft and combat vehicles. ∎

Messerschmidt Bf-109

This single-seat German fighter was extremely effective in **World War II** (1939–45). While being developed in the 1930s, a model of the Me 109 set an air speed record of 481mph. More than 30,000 Me 109s—commonly called Messerschmidts—were

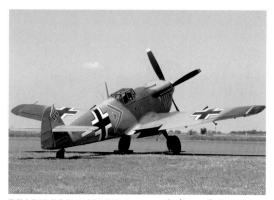

READY FOR ACTION Germany's finest fighter aircraft in World War II was the Messerschmidt, marked with a Nazi swastika on its tail; on the fuselage is the black and white symbol, termed a *Balkankreuz*, used to identify German aircraft and vehicles.

M

V-2 MISSILE

In mid-1944, Nazi Germany launched "V-weapons" against London and Paris. These rockets were named *Vergeltungswafen*, meaning "Revenge Weapons." More than 16,500 V-1s were launched, carrying 1,800-pound bombs and flying at 400mph, but many were shot down. V-1s used an innovative jet engine, but the V-2 was a true ballistic rocket, capable of flight outside earth's atmosphere. The V-2 had a 2,000-pound bomb, flew at 4,000mph, and there was no defense against it. Approximately 1,200 V-2s were fired at London.

produced for the German *Luftwaffe* (air force) during the war.

The Me 109 escorted German heavy bombers on raids, protecting them against enemy fighters. Operating over German-held territory, Me 109s rose to attack enemy bombers and their fighter escorts. They also took part in strikes on enemy shipping, troops, emplacements, and equipment.

Powered by an 1,800hp Daimler-Benz engine, the Me 109 had a maximum speed of more than 350mph and was armed with one 30mm or 20mm cannon and two 13mm machine guns. The Me 109 was the most common German fighter of World War II. ■

Mexican-American War

Also called the Mexican War, this conflict resulted mainly from Mexico's opposition to the U.S. 1845 annexation of the Republic of Texas, which had won its independence from Mexico in 1836.

In 1846, the U.S. attempted to negotiate the purchase of California and New Mexico from Mexico, which refused. American troops were moved into a disputed area near the Rio Grande, and the Mexican army attempted to force them out. After fighting began, the U.S. declared war, winning a series of battles fought in Texas, California, and New Mexico. At Monterrey and Buena Vista in Mexico, American forces under Zachary Taylor defeated Mexico's commander—and its president—Antonio Lopéz de Santa Anna. Other American military expeditions occupied weakly defended California and New Mexico.

Early in 1847, U.S. commander-in-chief Winfield Scott landed an army at Veracruz and drove toward the capital, Mexico City. After a series of battles culminating in the capture of the fortress of Chapultepec, Scott marched into Mexico City on September 14, 1847. For the first time in history, the American flag was raised in triumph over a foreign capital. The war ended in 1848, and the peace treaty brought vast western regions under U.S. control, including most of California, Utah, Nevada, Arizona, and New Mexico. ■

Mexican War of Independence

Liberty-minded Mexicans in the early 19th century demanded that Spain grant self-government and a redistribution of land and recognize equality of the races–Spanish, Indian, and mestizos (mixed blood).

In 1810, an uprising inspired by parish priest Hidalgo y Costilla resulted in the massacre of many of Mexico's upper class. In the end, the rebellion was crushed, and the colonial government triumphed in the years from 1810–15, as Hidalgo was captured and executed.

For years, Mexico continued to seethe under Spanish colonial rule, and guerrilla bands kept parts of the country troubled and dangerous. A republican revolution in Spain during the **Napoleonic Wars** helped open the way for Mexican independence. Unsupported by embattled Spain, Mexico's colonial government was weak and could

A STRONGPOINT FALLS In 1848, during the Mexican-American war, victorious American troops march into Churubusco, once a Mexican army stronghold just south of Mexico City.

MISSILES, SATELLITES

Satellites that orbit the earth are as important for preventing war as they are for guiding **intercontinental ballistic missiles** toward a target. Satellite cameras are "spies in the sky," monitoring the movements of the smallest military forces, thus making it difficult to start a war by surprise.

Even an unexpected attack by thousands of guided missiles would be observed immediately by satellites, and a warning beamed to the nation under attack, which would then launch its own missiles. Early-warning defense systems with satellites standing watch hundreds of miles above the earth deter even the strongest nuclear power from taking the offensive because the counterattack would be as devastating as the initial attack. The North American Air Defense Command (NORAD), based in Denver, controls a world-wide early-warning system of **radar** stations, satellites, and aircraft.

Laser-guided firing systems and computerized communications that determine the guided missile's accuracy and choice of targets depend on data from satellites. Some guided missiles have a range of more than 7,500 miles and carry multiple nuclear or conventional warheads, each of them hundreds of times more powerful than the **atomic bombs** dropped on Japan in **World War II** (1939–45).

In 1988, at the height of the Cold War, more than 20,000 warheads were in the U.S. and Soviet arsenals—9,789 U.S. and 10,595 Soviet. The U.S. had 2,002 missile "launchers," which included submarines, missile silos, mobile vehicles, and long-range bombers. The U.S.S.R. had 2,503 launchers. Many more missiles and launchers also belonged to additional nations that were allied with one side or the other.

At the start of the 21st century a strategic-defense technology, using satellites in the system, was being developed to intercept and destroy enemy missiles before they could reach their targets.

Congreve rockets were used by mid-1800s militaries, as seen in this 1845 image showing a demonstration of the missile. The rockets referred to in the "Star-spangled Banner" were Congreve rockets fired from British ships in Baltimore harbor in the War of 1812.

Lockheed Martin Milstar FV4 satellite, just prior to shipment to Cape Canaveral, Florida, for launching into space.

This modern Multiple Launch Rocket System, mounted on a tracked vehicle, can fire artillery rockets or missiles with explosive warheads.

A Tomahawk cruise missile is launched from the USS *Philippine Sea* in a strike on terrorist positions in the 2001 campaign against the Taliban regime in Afghanistan.

The U.S. Navy's Standard Missile is used against enemy aircraft, missiles, and ships.

M

not resist opposition. By 1821 an alliance of conservatives and guerrillas established what was intended to be the Mexican Empire with a constitutional monarch of its own.

Mexico was now independent of Spain, but she would have many more years of struggle before a stable, though autocratic, national government was established. ■

Mines, Land and Naval

Land mines are defensive weapons, usually buried and concealed, that explode when stepped on or driven over. Land mines block roads or protect disputed ground from being readily crossed by an enemy.

Small anti-personnel mines are designed to injure or kill the soldier who steps on one or who trips over a booby-trap wire that sets off a mine hidden nearby. Some antipersonnel mines spring into the air when activated and explode at waist level.

Extremely powerful antitank mines for disabling tanks or vehicles detonate only when a heavy weight goes over them. In the late 20th century, methods were developed to sow mines in the rear of enemy territory. These mines would be placed by using artillery fire, launching systems, and airdrops from **helicopters**.

Naval mines are underwater explosives

"ATTENTION! MINES!" World War II mines and antipersonnel devices are displayed alongside a skull-and-bones warning sign that alerts German soldiers to a minefield.

intended to damage passing vessels. These are either "contact" or "influence" mines. Contact mines explode when a vessel runs into them; influence mines are detonated by sensors affected by magnetics or the sound of an engine or by water-pressure changes caused by passing vessels. Naval mines can be moored to the floor of a sea, bay, or river, or they can drift with the tide into an enemy harbor or toward their fleet.

At the start of the 21st century, many countries in the world were plagued by millions of mines remaining from regional wars. Despite international programs to remove these mines, thousands of people were killed and injured by them every year. ■

Mongol Conquests

The Mongol Wars (1214–1402) were a series of conflicts brought on by the aggression of Mongol warriors led by **Genghis Khan** and his descendants.

A people from the wind-swept plains and mountains of Central Asia, the Mongols won repute as acrobatic riders skilled with a short bow.

In the 13th century, fierce Mongol horsemen invaded China, Japan, India, Persia, the Near East, and even reached the Danube River in eastern Europe. Kublai Khan was the Mongol emperor of China by 1260, establishing his capital in Beijing. The vast Mongol empire eventually reached from Europe to Japan.

Tamerlane, a descendant of Genghis Khan, conquered parts of Russia, India, and the Near East in the late 14th century. He was notorious for barbaric cruelty to the peoples he attacked. Other Mongol leaders were more humane, however, some guaranteeing freedom of religion and forbidding their men to massacre an enemy unless it was necessary for ultimate victory.

The Mongols became divided, as various leaders assumed regional power and fought with one another. The **"Golden Horde"** was a Mongol force that warred

with Russia and with other Mongols, including Tamerlane, until they were finally defeated by European armies in 1491.

By the 17th century, the Manchus of northeast Asia were conquering China and attacking Mongolia itself. In the West, Russia was rising to power, forcing the once-powerful Mongols into subjugation and ending their centuries of military and political dominance. ■

Musket

This term for the favorite military firearm from the late 16th to the mid-19th century was originally used for the smallest cannon of the 15th century. It comes from the Italian *moschetto*, meaning sparrow hawk.

Until the early 17th century, the main shoulder-held firearm was the arquebus, which was light enough not to need the support of a rest. The arquebus used a matchlock firing mechanism, which involved the arquebusier slowly pulling the gun's trigger to bring a burning match in contact with the black powder in the firing pan. The early musket was also fitted with a matchlock, but was heavier than the arquebus and longer-barrelled, so it required a rest when being fired. Some muskets had a crew of two men to handle the weapon and ammunition. The musket had more hitting-power than the arquebus, which it replaced during the 17th century.

Later musket designs used the more dependable flintlock firing mechanism, becoming lighter and easier to handle. From the 18th century onward, the term musket generally referred to shoulder-fired guns that used the flintlock firing mechanism. Muskets were "muzzle-loaders," meaning the powder charge and lead ball were loaded from the front end of the barrel and pushed down into place with a ramrod. The musket had a lethal range of about 200 yards, but it was not accurate.

Military firing (musketry) was by massed soldiers standing in long ranks, their muskets simply pointed in the direction of the enemy, not aimed. One of the most famous muskets was the Redcoat smoothbore "Brown Bess," which was the standard firearm of the British Army from 1730–1830. Most army muskets were "smoothbores," without **rifling,** which is a series of long spiral grooves cut into the inside of the gun barrel. Rifling causes the bullet to spin and gives it far better accuracy. Smoothbore muskets were inaccurate beyond 50 yards, but they were preferred by the military because they could be loaded and fired much more rapidly than rifles. (Muzzle-loading early rifles were longer than smoothbores and took a bullet that fit tightly into the barrel).

In the hands of trained soldiers standing in ranks, muskets offered firepower that came from their speed of firing enmasse, not from accuracy.

Ammunition improvements in the mid-19th century permitted the development of rifled muskets. These weapons were far more deadly than smoothbores.

In the second half of the 19th century, breech-loading rifles became the standard firearm carried by every well-equipped infantry soldier. ■

A CONTINENTAL
A soldier of the American regular army in the Revolutionary War rams home a cartridge as he reloads his musket; rebel regulars were termed "Continentals," because their regiments were available for service anywhere in the colonies rather than in just their home state.

N-O

Napoleonic Wars

From 1792–1802, coalitions of European powers fought against Revolutionary France, which saw the rise of **Napoleon Bonaparte** as general and military dictator. Napoleon declared himself emperor in 1804, and France's wars were named for him until he was defeated in 1815.

France had a mighty army and powerful navy as she battled Britain, Austria, Russia, Sweden, Naples, and Prussia. France suffered defeats in great sea battles at Trafalgar and Finisterre Cape in 1805, but Napoleon was successful on land, defeating Austria at Austerlitz that year. His 1806–07 campaigns against Prussia and Russia were victorious, but his army became bogged down in Spain after 1808. There, he was fighting the British as well as Spanish rebels, who opposed Napoleon's naming of his brother, Joseph, as king of Spain.

Napoleon invaded Russia in 1812, but could not overcome the Russian spirit, great distances, and brutal winter. He held the field at Borodino in 1812 and captured Moscow, but at great loss.

That winter Napoleon was forced to retreat, closely pursued by the Russians. The withdrawal was disaster, costing the lives of 400,000 French and their allies, almost the entire invading army.

Napoleon was defeated on every front, and Paris fell in May 1814. Napoleon abdicated and was exiled to Elba, but returned in 1815 to recover his throne. Warfare raged in what is known as "Napoleon's Hundred Days," ending with defeat at Waterloo, Belgium, on June 18. Napoleon was again exiled, this time for life, and the Napoleonic Wars came to a close. ∎

Needlegun

This rifle, which appeared in the mid-19th century, had an ignition mechanism that fired a bullet by striking it with a spring-loaded needle. Pulling the trigger struck the needle against the bullet's base.

The early needlegun used a bullet with an explosive charge in its base, which fired upon impact. These "pinfire" cartridges opened the way for the rapid development of ammunition. They became known as "center-fire" bullets because the needle struck the center of their base to detonate the charge. The needlegun led to many firearm improvements that soon followed.

The needlegun was a "breechloader"– the bullet inserted from the back of the

EMPEROR AND GENERAL
Napoleon Bonaparte rides at the head of his general staff as his army marches alongside during the 1814 campaign in France; Bonaparte's troops had great fighting spirit, and his marshals and generals were among the best battlefield commanders of the day.

gun, not down the muzzle. Bolt-action breechloaders fired several times faster than a muzzle-loader. Also, while the muzzle-loader required a soldier to stand up while loading, the breechloader could be loaded while the soldier was safely lying down. The needlegun was adopted by the Prussian army in 1840 and used effectively against small German states over the next 20 years. Carried by government troops late in the Italian Wars of Independence from Austria (1821–70), breechloaders devastated insurgent forces that were using mainly muzzle-loaders.

Later breechloaders had internal magazines with several bullets, which were inserted into the firing chamber by the bolt action. This "repeating rifle" offered dramatically increased firepower, changing the face of war. ■

Nigerian Civil War

Also called the Biafran War, this civil conflict resulted from internal political strife in Nigeria, which became independent from Britain in 1960.

One of the largest countries in Africa, Nigeria's population in the mid-1960s was almost 70 million, divided into several regions. At that time, the mainly Christian Ibo people objected to persecution of Christians by some Muslims who were in power. In 1966, a coup led by Ibos assassinated the elected prime minister and other officials and established a military government. It was quickly overthrown by officers of the northern Hausa tribe, mainly Muslims. Again, the Nigerian leader was murdered. Mobs took to the streets, each slaughtering members of other tribes and faiths. The Nigerian central government had become helpless.

In May 1967, the southeast region dominated by Ibos declared independence as the Republic of Biafra. Fighting began between Nigeria's government troops and the Biafrans, whose capital, Enugu, fell in October. The political association of African countries, the Organization of African Unity, tried without success to mediate a peace. Fighting raged until January 1970, when the isolated and blockaded Biafrans were forced to surrender after starvation had killed thousands in addition to the casualties from warfare.

Before the civil war, the Nigerian federal army was only a ceremonial force of 7,000, and by 1970 it numbered more than 200,000—a crushing expense for this young country. ■

Norman Conquest

The Battle of Hastings in 1066 was the most decisive engagement ever fought on English soil. King Harold II, Saxon lord of England, was fighting an invasion of Vikings in the North of the country, when Normans invaded in the South. Led by Duke William of Normandy, 7,000 fighting men had sailed across the English Channel and landed at Pevensey, Sussex.

Harold defeated the Vikings—the Scandinavian people from whom the Normans were descended—and immediately

NORMAN HORSEMEN The Normans who invaded England in 1066 included many horsemen; they attacked and defeated the Saxons, who were famed for wielding battleaxes.

Seen through a single-tube night vision goggle, this U.S. Marine prepares for a raid on a suspected Al Qaeda position in Afghanistan in 2002.

A U.S. Army soldier uses state-of-the-art night vision goggles.

O

marched southward against William. Also leading 7,000 men, Harold took up a position on Senlac Hill at Hastings, blocking the road to London. William charged with his mounted armored **knights,** who were repulsed by Saxons wielding spears and broad axes. The Saxons counterattacked too soon, however, and were bloodied by the knights, who rallied and held the Norman center. Under a rain of Norman arrows, the Saxons again took up defensive positions, standing their ground against repeated charges by the knights.

That evening, the Normans appeared to be withdrawing. The Saxons again were overconfident, breaking ranks, and charging into a trap. The Normans turned on them, and Harold fell with an arrow in his eye, a mortal wound. The leaderless Saxons were defeated. The Norman duke, who became known as William the Conqueror, was crowned king of England. ■

Opium Wars

These two conflicts led to Western nations dominating trade with China and laid the foundation for 150 years of Chinese resentment against the West. The first Opium War sprang from Chinese objections to British importation of illegal opium, a powerful narcotic. The Chinese tried to halt the opium trade, which turned many people into addicts. The British refused, however, for they were prospering from the exchange of tea from China for opium from India.

When the Chinese forcefully took possession of opium stored in British warehouses in the trading port of Canton, hostilities broke out. The small but well-armed British force won a decisive victory.

In 1842, peace terms were finally settled, compelling the Chinese to give control of five seaports to the British. At the same time, other Western nations made similar demands on defeated China. Furthermore, Westerners who were accused of a crime in China would no longer be subject to Chinese courts and could only be tried by other Westerners.

In 1856, the French and British trumped up reasons for another such conflict in order to expand their trading rights.

The second Opium War resulted in another easy victory. Now, the Westerners demanded freedom of movement for Christian missionaries in China. Several more sea ports were forcibly opened to Western trade, and opium was legalized in China.

When the rulers of China refused the terms, Westerners attacked Beijing and burned the emperor's summer palace. The Chinese had no other choice than to accept humiliating peace terms forced upon them by the Westerners. ■

PUNISHING CANTON A British fleet bombards the city of Canton at the outbreak of the first Opium War in 1839; the British and other Westerners attacked the city in order to force favorable trading concessions from the Chinese government.

86

P-Q

P-51 Fighter Plane

The "Mustang," as this American fighter was called, was one of the most important combat aircraft of **World War II** (1939–45), with more than 14,000 built during the war.

Serious bomber losses over Axis-held Europe in 1943 made it essential to put a fast, long-range fighter escort into service. The P-51 Mustang was the answer. The best of these planes had a range of 900 miles, so they could stay with the heavy bombers during a mission deep into enemy territory. The Mustang was the fastest piston-engine fighter plane of the World War II, with some models capable of speeds up to 480mph.

By mid-1944, with swarms of Mustangs taking on German fighters, the balance of air power over Europe shifted dramatically in favor of the Allies. Heavy losses were incurred on both sides, but the Allies kept building more planes and training new pilots, while Germany's *Luftwaffe* (air force) could not replace lost planes or pilots fast enough.

The dependable Mustang was also an important aircraft in the first part of the **Korean War** (1950–53), until the much-faster jet fighter began to dominate combat. ■

Panzer

Meaning "armor," the term panzer referred to German tanks and other armored vehicles, and also was the term for armored battle-formations that gave Germany victory in the first years of **World War II** (1939–45).

Panzer divisions supported by air assaults punched holes in slow-moving enemy defenses, through which motorized infantry surged, trapping large pockets of defenders.

Although Germany had almost no tanks in **World War I** (1914–18), by 1939 her military leaders created large, well-trained armored formations. German tanks led the **blitzkrieg,** or "lightning war," that swept across France and the Low Countries in 1940 and forced their surrender, driving the British army from the European continent.

Massed formations of speedy, hard-hitting panzers at first vanquished all-comers in European and in North African campaigns.

The Allies learned from German tank design and tactics and eventually developed their own first-rate armor that by the end of World War II met the panzers on equal terms. ■

PANZER TANKS
German armor swings into action during the Russian campaign of World War II; the Russians built their own excellent tanks and developed armored units and battlefield tactics that were a match for the Germans.

P

The percussion lock of a British pistol of the 1840s.

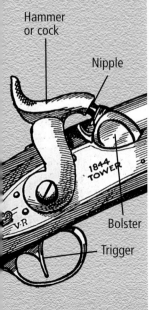

Hammer or cock

Nipple

1844 TOWER

V·R

Bolster

Trigger

Peloponnesian Wars

In the 5th century BC, the Greek city-state of Sparta rose to power as a rival to Athens. Sparta and Athens waged a war that is named for the mountainous peninsula where Sparta is located, called Peloponnese.

The First Peloponnesian War (458–446BC) ended in an inconclusive truce. After 15 years of uneasy peace, Athens sent out a great fleet to subdue the island of Sicily, only to find the Spartans had allied with the Sicilians. The Athenian expedition was destroyed, and conflict between the two city-states resumed as the Second Peloponnesian War (431–404BC).

In 405BC, a powerful Spartan fleet aided by Persia defeated the Athenian fleet at Aegospotami. A year later, Athens fell, her imperial power broken forever. This conflict marked the beginning of the decline of ancient Greek civilization. ∎

Persian Gulf War

This 1991 conflict between Iraq and a coalition of 32 members of the United Nations—including the United States, Britain, Egypt, France, and Saudi Arabia—began with Iraq's August 1990 invasion of neighboring Kuwait.

Iraq, which had long claimed Kuwait belonged to her, accused Kuwait of illegally pumping oil from an Iraqi oil field. Both nations are rich in oil. The UN Security Council called for Iraq to withdraw, and coalition troops moved into Saudi Arabia, also adjacent to Iraq. The UN set a January 1991 deadline for a peaceful withdrawal of Iraqi troops from Kuwait. The Iraqis refused, however, and the campaign, "Operation Desert Storm," was launched by the coalition on January 18th.

With U.S. leadership the coalition's massive air war quickly destroyed Iraq's military and civil infrastructure. In late February, coalition forces invaded Kuwait and Iraq and, in just four days, encircled and defeated the Iraqi occupying army and liberated Kuwait. By the time the coalition declared a cease-fire on February 28th, most of the Iraqi forces in Kuwait had either surrendered or fled.

Peace terms that included regular UN inspections of Iraqi weapons production were agreed to, but Iraq's president, Saddam Hussein, did all in his power to frustrate inspections. In 1993, the United States, France, and Britain launched punitive air and missile strikes against Iraq, which continued to resist inspections. Trouble continued when an Iraqi troop buildup near the Kuwait border in 1994 compelled the U.S. to send forces to the area. Iraqi resistance to weapons inspections led to a long-term U.S. military presence in the Persian Gulf, and periodic bombing raids continued against Iraq into 2001. ∎

Peter I, the Great (1672–1725)

One of Russia's most accomplished leaders, Peter the Great brought his empire to new heights of influence and power. As czar (emperor), he was a visionary reformer and a successful military commander.

With ice-bound coasts in the North and

RUSSIA'S BRILLIANT CZAR Peter the Great is portrayed with sword and cannon that symbolize his military successes, which expanded the Russian empire from Europe to the Pacific.

PISTOL

First invented in the 14th century, this short-barrelled firearm is designed to be fired with one hand. Pistols came into wide use as military firearms in the mid-16th century, employing the wheel-lock firing system, which ignited the charge by a spark.

Early on, pistols were carried for self-defense, and for the first time a physically weaker individual could confront someone much stronger on equal terms. Pistols became favored by cavalry, who used them in a method of attack known as the "caracole." This was a charge that stopped just short of the enemy, followed by the massed firing of pistols, and then withdrawal to reload while other cavalry did the same.

Pistols developed parallel with shoulder-held firearms, as improved ignition and loading systems made them increasingly effective in battle. They came to be divided into two main classes: the revolver and the automatic. The revolver has a cylinder with several chambers, each holding one cartridge, which move into firing position when the trigger is pulled. The automatic feeds cartridges into the firing chamber from a magazine, in a process powered by the force of the pistol's recoil on firing.

Among the most popular automatic pistols of the American military was the .45 caliber manufactured by Colt Industries.

A late 16th century armored cavalryman "presents and gives fyre" with a wheel-lock pistol. Carried in a pair of holsters in front of the saddle, pistols remained an important part of a cavalryman's armament until the 20th century.

Flintlock pistols, elegantly decorated, with carrying bags.

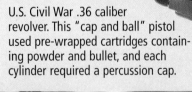

U.S. Civil War .36 caliber revolver. This "cap and ball" pistol used pre-wrapped cartridges containing powder and bullet, and each cylinder required a percussion cap.

M-9 Beretta semi-automatic pistol with 15-shot magazine; this weapon is often carried by law enforcement officers and military aviators.

A U.S. sergeant fires a 9mm pistol during combat team competitions in 1996.

P

POLE ARMS

Pole arms is a term for "staff weapons," meaning they are edged weapons mounted to the end of wooden poles, or staffs. Sometimes fitted to steel shafts, the bladed head of a staff weapon could be attached by such methods as lacing, nailing or riveting. Later, most had sockets that fit tightly over the shaft, with long steel strips called langets that protected the shaft from being cut in combat. The Swiss armies of the 15th and 16th centuries were noted for their ferocious attacks with halberds that cut through the strongest armor.

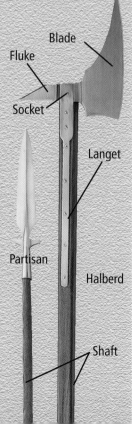

Blade

Fluke

Socket

Langet

Partisan

Halberd

Shaft

East, and landlocked borders in the South, Russia was ever in search of warm-water ports. Russian diplomacy and war have been dictated by this long-standing objective. Peter acquired ports in the Baltic Sea, and his military successes against the Swedish empire won him enduring fame. He did much to make his country a formidable power in Europe and Central Asia.

From youth, Peter was fascinated by mathematics, sailing ships, navigation, and fortifications. As a prince, he traveled and studied, sometimes working incognito as an apprentice ship's carpenter in the Lowlands and Britain to find out how they built their vessels. When he became czar, Peter sent young Russian nobles out to learn what they could of Western ways.

As a diplomat, Peter made shrewd alliances against the Swedes in the North and Ottoman Turks in the South. The 21-year **Great Northern War** (1700–21) was his supreme accomplishment. Allied with Saxony and Denmark-Norway against the dominant Swedes, Peter won the battle of Poltava in 1709, breaking Sweden's military strength. He also built the first Russian navy and won the first great Russian sea victory—against the Swedes at the battle of Gangut in 1714.

When Peter died in 1725, Russia was one of the mightiest nations of Europe, stretching to the Pacific Ocean. ∎

Phalanx

This tactical formation of tightly packed spearmen took shape in ancient Greece during the 7th century BC. Previously, battles had involved single-combat between individual heroes, and the development of the mighty phalanx transformed warfare.

The individual soldier was a hoplite, a free man from the property-owning, landed class. Armed with a long pike, a **shield,** and

ALEXANDER'S PHALANX A Macedonian phalanx, with ranks of long pikes presented, is ready to engage Indian soldiers and war elephants in northern India during the 3rd century BC.

a sword, the hoplite had only three feet of room in which to move. There was little use for the sword, for there was no room to swing it. The pike—some projecting forward more than 18 feet from each of as many as eight successive rows of hoplites—was what made the phalanx irresistible as it marched slowly against an enemy. The phalanx advanced in step, their pace sounded out by the shrill of a flute.

Cavalry could do nothing against this barrier of spears, and arrows were deflected by the forest of upraised pikes in the rearward ranks. If, however, an enemy was willing to charge, mass for mass, the advantage almost always went to the Greek phalanx and their hedgehog of spears. There was little need for maneuvering as long as both armies agreed to crash headlong into each other in the middle of the field.

The phalanx dominated infantry warfare until 200BC, when Romans developed the **legion,** which was more flexible and maneuverable. Early phalanxes numbered about 200 men, later growing to 5,000 strong. ∎

Plate Armor

After 1300, the development of powerful archery forced the counter-development of plate armor, usually of iron or steel.

Plate armor was effective against edged weapons, and as crossbows and **longbows**

PRISONERS OF WAR

Soldiers captured during a war are known as prisoners of war (P.O.W.s). Civilian prisoners do not fall into this category.

Until the 16th century, prisoners captured in battle might be put to death or sold into slavery. Before the modern era, prisoners were considered spoils of war. They were forced to become servants, field slaves, or laborers in mines or on public works. They were seldom kept imprisoned for long because of the high cost of feeding, housing, and guarding them.

Later wars, fought by nations for specific political or economic purposes, were not intended to wipe out an enemy. Those conflicts saw the exchange of prisoners under mutually agreed-upon terms or at the end of hostilities. In the 18th–19th centuries, prisoners of war were often sent back to their own lines on condition they give their promise, "parole," not to return to action until an enemy prisoner of equal rank was officially exchanged–private for private, general for general.

Yet there was always the need for temporary prisoner-of-war camps, where conditions were often unhealthy and sometimes brutal, even into the late 20th century. Racial and religious hostility, civil strife, and old hatreds too often brought out the lust for revenge against the prisoner.

After the 19th century, international agreements were reached to govern the humane treatment of prisoners of war, who were often kept in closely guarded camps surrounded by walls and fences. Modern P.O.W.s have certain rights, including the right to medical treatment and protection from further attack or insults. They are not considered culprits who deserve to be punished, but rather as detainees being kept from further involvement in the war.

The P.O.W.'s rights are encompassed by the Third Geneva (Switzerland) Convention of 1949, the terms of which must be made available to prisoners in their own language.

American prisoners suffered inhumane conditions on British prison ships moored in New York City harbor during the Revolutionary War.

A Union prisoner is shot for straying too near the fence, known as the "dead line," at the notorious Confederate prison camp in Andersonville, Georgia.

In 1942, World War II American prisoners of the Japanese were forced on a long journey from Bataan, in the Philippines; so many prisoners died that it was known as the "Bataan Death March."

Iraqi troops are captured by United Nations armor in the Desert Storm campaign of 1991.

British soldiers escort captured German "Afrika Korps" troops in the North African desert in 1942.

P

PROJECTILES AND AMMUNITION

A warrior of ancient times, protected by his shield, is about to hurl a stone from a sling. Ancient armies often had large numbers of slingers using this very effective weapon

A military projectile is anything that is launched at a target, and can be a stone, bullet, or a self-propelled rocket. Early projectiles were rocks hurled from a slingshot, spears thrown by hand, and arrows shot from bows.

Ammunition can mean the missiles or projectiles that are fired from a bow or firearm. Today, ammunition generally refers to bullets or shells of various sizes and the explosives required to fire them.

Early cannons fired spears and arrows as well as stones, and later shot specially made balls of iron. These balls could be heavy for destroying fortifications, or small and bundled together like "grapes" in order to kill soldiers. Until the mid-19th century, the prime shoulder-held firearm was the **musket,** which fired a lead ball. The rifle came next, eventually using bullets that had their own firing charge in a brass cartridge.

Artillery pieces by the thousands dominated **World War I** (1914–19). During the 1916 Battle of the Somme, British artillery fired four million rounds, 125 times the amount of ammunition fired by the Union army at the 1863 Battle of Gettysburg in the American Civil War.

In the late 20th century, rockets became potent projectiles, especially those fired by hand-held anti-tank and anti-aircraft weapons. At the turn of the 21st century, mobile rocket-launchers that could be driven into action were capable of firing hundreds of rockets within just a few seconds.

World War I American artillerymen load and fire a rapid-fire field gun amidst piles of ejected brass shell casings.

Paper cartridges held gunpowder and a musket ball for firearms of the Revolutionary War; the paper was torn open, and the powder, ball and paper placed down the gun barrel.

American .45 caliber cartridges for rifles and pistols in the "Old West" of the late 1800s.

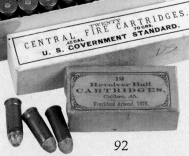

TWENTY
CENTRAL FIRE CARTRIDGES.
.45 CAL   70 GRS.
U.S. GOVERNMENT STANDARD.

12
Revolver Ball
CARTRIDGES.
Calibre .45.
Frankford Arsenal. 1878.

A British cannonball of the late 1700s, marked with the "Broad Arrow" as government property; right, an artillery shell, which was to be filled with gunpowder.

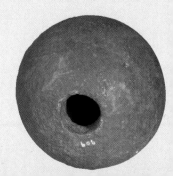

became ever more powerful, new-made plate armor was "proofed" by firing at it from various distances to test its strength. The advent of firearms by the 15th century meant the end of plate armor, which could not stop a bullet.

Highly-decorated plate armor known as "parade" armor, was worn for ceremonial occasions rather than battle.

In the 17th century, upper-body plate armor and helmets were worn by some cavalrymen and arquebusiers (gunners). Plate armor was worn into the 19th century by heavy cavalry, such as the French cuirassiers, whose torsos were covered with a plate "cuirass," their heads protected by helmets. ■

Punic Wars

The Roman Republic and the North African state of Carthage were vying for supreme power in the Mediterranean region. This struggle brought on the First Punic War (264–241BC). The Punic Wars were three conflicts that together lasted almost 120 years.

Carthage (now Tunisia) was the great sea power of the day, while Rome had the mightiest land army, but the Romans copied their enemy's naval methods and also gained supremacy over the seas. Rome emerged triumphant from each of the conflicts, also called the Carthaginian Wars.

The most outstanding military figure of the age was **Hannibal** of Carthage. In the Second Punic War (218–201BC), he invaded Italy, itself, defeating every **Roman army** sent against him. Rome forced Hannibal to leave Italy and defend his home city. Under the brilliant generalship of Publius Scipio, the Romans ultimately defeated Hannibal on his own soil.

In the Third Punic War (149–146BC), the victorious Romans ruthlessly laid waste to Carthage and turned the country into the Roman province of Africa. ■

Queen Anne's War

As the **War of the Spanish Succession** (1701–14) raged in Europe, it was also fought in colonial North America, pitting the British against the allied French and Spanish. In America, the war was known as Queen Anne's War, named after the reigning British queen.

The struggle also drew in the native tribes who chose sides according to their own key interests and friendships. In 1706, Spanish forces mounted an unsuccessful seaborne attack against Charleston, South Carolina. This attack was in reprisal for the 1702 sacking of St. Augustine, Florida, by Carolinian militia and their Indian allies.

As with most American colonial wars, the conflict was marked by cruel frontier raids and counter-raids. The 1703 massacre of settlers at Deerfield, Massachusetts, by the French and Indians remains one of the most enduring legacies of the war.

The largest battle was in 1710, when a British and colonial force of 4,000 captured the French stronghold of Port Royal on the Atlantic coast island of Acadia (Nova Scotia). A year later, a British and colonial expedition sailing up the Saint Lawrence River against the French at Quebec and Montreal was destroyed by a storm. More than 900 of the 5,000-man army drowned, and the invasion was called off. ■

WAR ELEPHANTS IN ITALY

In 218BC, the Carthaginian general, Hannibal, brought several war elephants across the Alps on his invasion of Italy in the Second Punic War. However impressive they might be, elephants proved of little military value to Hannibal.

R

Radar

"Radar" is an acronym for "radio detecting and ranging." An electronic system, radar uses radio waves to locate and track objects at a distance.

Radar was secretly developed by the British prior to **World War II** (1939–45). It measures the time required for a radio wave to travel from a transmitter to an object and return again. This measurement can tell the position, distance, and speed of an object, and also the direction it is moving. Originally known as RDF—radio direction finding—radar was crucial to locating and tracking German combat aircraft and bombers approaching Britain.

Radar was also used for aerial and marine navigation, aerial bombing, submarine detection, and for aiming artillery.

The soldier of the 21st century can be equipped with sophisticated radar that detects movement of vehicles under cover of darkness or in fog. By beaming microwaves off a target object, the spotter on the ground helps the combat pilot home in on his target. Radar can also be used from aircraft to study terrain by scanning with radar waves.

Radar is used in missile guidance systems and in anti-missile defenses. In addition to military uses, radar is employed for mapping, for studying atmospheric events, and as a tool for meteorologists—tracking storms, measuring precipitation, and locating regions of turbulence. ■

Railroads

The speed and power of the locomotive drastically changed warfare in the mid-19th century, as troops, equipment, and supplies were transported overnight to strategic positions.

The **U.S. Civil War** (1861–65) saw the first major use of the railroad in warfare. The Union's great advantage in locomotives, freight cars, and track was instrumental in final victory. By the 1870s, much of Europe was served by railroads, and in the regional wars of that time troop-movement and army mobilization depended on trains. Ownership of railroads and their fuel became, itself, a flash point for war. Locomotive boilers needed coal, so nations fought for coal mines to feed their industry and railroads.

In war, railroads were often the object of attack, as combatants tried to control or destroy them. Just as rivers and bridges were key strategic points, so were railroad lines, junctions, trestles, tunnels, and locomotives

EARLY RADAR
A five-man crew of U.S. Signal Corps soldiers operates a mobile radar system stationed on an Italian hillside during World War II; radar scans the skies and detects aircraft, thus warning of the approach of enemy warplanes.

manufacturing works. Armies aimed to capture enemy railroad networks and trains and also had to protect their own from attack.

Locomotives were also used as mobile platforms for "railway guns," some of the largest artillery pieces ever used. The mightest railway gun of all was the German "Gustav" cannon, weighing 1,350 tons. It was used as a siege weapon against the Russian city of Sevastopol in 1942.

Rifling

This is a system of spiral grooves inside a gun barrel, which impart a spin to the projectile when it is fired and improves accuracy. The grooves usually make one full turn over the length of the barrel. The spin gives the projectile—whether a bullet or a cannonball—stability in its trajectory.

A rifle is any firearm that has such grooves in its "bore," as the inside of the barrel is called. A firearm without rifling is termed a "smoothbore." Modern pistols, shoulder-held firearms, machine guns, and artillery pieces all are rifled, although the term "rifle" usually means the shoulder-held firearm.

RIFLED BARREL The spiral grooves—rifling—of this U.S. 8-inch howitzer are clearly visible inside the barrel.

The first known rifling dates to the late 15th century, but rifled guns did not come into wide use for another 300 years. The military generally used smoothbores, which were much faster to load. The extra length of the 18th-century rifle—which was muzzle-loading—made it difficult to ram down the ball in loading.

By the mid-19th century, most soldiers carried rifled firearms, which soon became breechloading—loaded from the back. In the 20th century, all military weapons were rifled. ■

Roman Army

As Rome rose to power in the 3rd century BC, her war making was methodical and scientific. The Romans were not only experts at conducting sieges and building siege engines such as battering rams, catapults, and fighting towers, but their own fortifications were extremely strong.

An enemy seldom caught the Romans unprepared for battle. A Roman army on campaign in hostile territory built a fortified camp wherever it stopped. These camps followed similar lines, and any soldier in the empire knew his duty in both construction and defense. Whether on campaign or stationed in a remote garrison protecting the frontier, the Roman soldier benefited from a well-ordered system of supply, sanitation, and even mail service. As a result, the **legions** were better fed and housed and were healthier than enemy warriors.

At the same time, tactics in battle were thoroughly drilled and understood by every man, down to the ordinary legionary. The Roman legionary used a short, thrusting sword (*gladius*) and a stout throwing spear (*pilum*) and employed a heavy **shield** (*scutum*).

At first, the Roman army was composed of loyal citizen-soldiers who fought for their country, then returned home when the war was won. Roman soldiers had a great confidence and unity that made them almost invincible. The empire

R

was weakened, however when non-Romans were hired instead of patriotic citizen soldiers.

The Roman army was organized in 100-man units, called centuries. These belonged to cohorts of 400–600 men, with 10 cohorts comprising a legion. At her height in the 1st century BC, Rome had as many as 30 legions round the empire—150,000 soldiers. They were supported by another 375,000 lightly armed troops and cavalry called auxiliaries, bringing Rome's total number of men under arms to more than half a million. ∎

Russian Civil War

This struggle tore revolutionary Russia apart, ending with the defeat of counter-revolutionary forces known as the "Whites."

The Whites opposed the 1917 Communist revolution that overthrew the czar (emperor) and established a government run by the Bolshevik party, identified as "Reds." The civil war was widespread throughout the former Russian empire—now divided up into regions governed by counsels known as "soviets"—but there were no major pitched battles.

The Reds were attacked on every side by a hodgepodge of opponents, including conservatives, anti-Communists, and the

MANCHURIAN WINTER Japanese troops on winter campaign at Haicheng in 1894, during the Russo-Japanese War.

nationalists. Added to these were several thousand American, British, Japanese, and French troops who briefly intervened in mid-1918 to keep the Russian front open against Germany, which was in the throes of **World War I** (1914–18). One American regiment suffered more than 500 casualties before the Allies withdrew in 1919.

The White armies took the offensive in several regions, but were they defeated by 1920. The presence of Western troops fighting with the Whites left long-lasting bitterness in the future Soviet Union. ∎

Russo-Japanese War

Japan's stunning victory in this war made her the first Asian nation to triumph over a European power.

Russian empire-building in the Far East created hostility with Japan. Both wanted to control Korea and Manchuria, and Russia had troops in Manchuria as well as a great naval base at Port Arthur. Japan demanded that Russia withdraw from Manchuria, and when this did not happen, Japan launched a surprise assault on Port Arthur in February 1904. The city fell after a year's siege.

Soon afterward, in February 1905, armies of more than 300,000 on each side met at Mukden in Manchuria. The result was a Japanese victory that cost 50,000 casualties, with the Russians losing twice as many.

Russian military leadership was incompetent, but the Japanese were modern in their equipment and war-making methods. The Japanese navy was especially successful, crushing a 45-ship Russian fleet in May 1905 at Tsushima Strait, between Japan and Korea. Only 12 Russian vessels escaped sinking or capture, while the Japanese lost only three torpedo boats. The war ended in this year.

Although Russia kept control of northern Manchuria after the war, Japan was on its way to becoming the leading military force in the Far East. ∎

Saladin (1137–93)

This is the Western name for Salah-ad-Din, the greatest Muslim hero in the 12th-century struggle with European crusaders for control of the Holy Land.

When Saladin came into power, thousands of Christians from the First and Second **Crusades** occupied much of the region, including Jerusalem. Of Kurdish descent, Saladin was sultan (ruler) of Syria, Egypt, Yemen, and Palestine. He inspired the Muslims to see the struggle against crusaders as a holy war, organizing schools to teach Muslim culture and faith and to discipline his fighters.

The hard-riding Saladin led his forces to victory after victory. His greatest triumph was the capture of Jerusalem in 1187, defeating the Franks, who had occupied the city for 88 years. A Third Crusade to recapture Jerusalem was immediately launched by the leading kings of Europe—including England's Richard I, the Lion Heart. Saladin was instrumental in thwarting them, however, and the Crusade failed.

It is noteworthy that crusader conquests usually resulted in great bloodshed and massacres, but Saladin's victories ended with chivalry and good will toward the defeated. ∎

Samurai

A member of the Japanese warrior class, the samurai was an aristocrat who strictly followed Bushido, a "code of warriors" set down by sacred tradition.

Bushido has varied in content over the centuries, but its central theme is to promote fighting spirit, athletic ability, and courage. The code also demands modest living, kindness, and unswerving honesty as well as respect for the family, especially for one's parents. The samurai had to be the perfect gentleman, an example of all that was virtuous. Later, obedience to government authority became an essential aspect of the Bushido code.

The samurai caste came to power in Japan in the 11th century and dominated until the mid-18th century. The samurai was famous for his ornate armor and curved, two-handed sword. When fighting men of courage and ability were needed, the samurai caste was open to all who qualified. By the 17th century, 200

SAMURAI IN COMBAT
Swinging the long-bladed sword for which his warrior class was famous, a samurai fights at Kumamoto Castle during one of Japan's many civil wars.

S

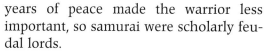

SEMINOLE WAR CHIEF
One of the most able native chiefs ever to fight the U.S. government, Osceola (1800?–38) led his outnumbered Seminole warriors in Florida during the 1820s and 1830s. He led resistance to his Seminoles being forced onto reservations; his capture came in 1837, when he was tricked by a pretended flag of truce. Osceola died in prison soon afterwards.

years of peace made the warrior less important, so samurai were scholarly feudal lords.

In the 19th century, Bushido became the basis for ethical training in Japanese society, requiring loyalty and sacrifice for the sake of the emperor, who was considered divine. ■

Seminole Wars

The 40-year struggle by the Seminole people of Florida against the U.S. government was the longest of America's Indian Wars.

The Seminoles were one of the South's "Five Civilized Tribes"–along with the Creeks, Choctaw, Cherokee, and Chickasaw. These peoples owned land the government wanted to give to white settlers. General Andrew Jackson moved troops into Seminole country in 1817, claiming he was hunting for runaway slaves. The Seminoles, who had intermarried with former slaves, resisted fiercely, and Jackson destroyed their villages. His forces even occupied territory belonging to Spain, which possessed most of Florida.

As a result of the First Seminole War (1816–18), Spain was forced to cede Florida to the U.S.

The Second Seminole War (1835–42) began when the tribe refused to be forced out of lands the government had reserved for them near Lake Okeechobee. Their brilliant chief, Osceola, led 1,000 men in small, but bitter battles against 5,000 invading government troops. Osceola was tricked in 1837, taken prisoner under a flag of truce, and without him Seminole resistance was weakened. Although many fled deep into the wild, most were forced westward onto reservations.

The Third Seminole War (1855–58) was started in 1855 to round up all remaining Seminoles, but there was little fighting. In the end, the government paid the last Seminoles to go West peacefully. ■

Seven Years' War

A wide-ranging conflict, the Seven Years' War (1756–63) left Great Britain with the world's strongest colonial empire, and Prussia, under **Frederick the Great,** became a major power.

Britain, Prussia, and Portugal fought France, Austria, Sweden, Spain, Poland, and Russia. The war resulted from Austria's attempts to regain territory which it had lost to Prussia in the **War of the Austrian Succession** (1740–48). Known in North America as the **French and Indian War,** the Seven Years' War ended with Britain capturing the vast expanse of French Canada and Spanish Florida. The British also won major land and sea victories in campaigns for India and the West Indies. In America, the fall of Fort Louisburg in 1758 and Quebec in 1759 were the most important campaigns won by the British.

SEMINOLE DEFEAT In 1837, 500 Seminoles were overmatched by 1,000 U.S. troops at Lake Okeechobee, Florida; fought near a fort, it was one of the largest clashes of the Seminole wars.

The war's greatest land engagements took place in Europe. At first, Prussia won brilliant victories against great odds, but in 1760–61 Prussia suffered several severe defeats. The withdrawal of Russia from the war in 1762 compelled Austria to make peace terms, which prevented it from regaining the lost territory from Prussia. ■

Sherman Tank

Built by the U.S. during **World War II** (1939–45), the Sherman was a medium-size tank with a 76mm gun. In the middle years of the war, it was rapidly manufactured for the British, who were engaged in North Africa and desperately needed armor.

More than 49,000 Sherman tanks were made, making them the principle tank in the Allied armies.

Late in the war, however, the Sherman tank had insufficient armor to stand up to the powerful new "tank-killing" **Tiger tanks** of Nazi Germany. Victory in Europe was more the result of sheer numbers of Allied tanks, not superiority in machines, which the Germans held. ■

THROUGH THE RUBBLE Machine gunner on alert, a Sherman tank advances with American infantry in the ruined French city of St. Lo.

Shield

A defensive weapon, the shield came in many shapes and sizes, depending on the method of warfare, tactics, or whether the fighter was on horseback or in a mass of infantry.

Shields were made of tough hide, wood, or metal, usually painted and decorated, perhaps with the owner's personal design, a family crest, the number of a military unit, or the sacred symbols of a people. Shields were used to force adversaries back or to divert blows and follow up with a counterblow.

Shields often had a metal boss in the center, which could be used for striking at an enemy.

Heroes in ancient Greece used great oval shields, and Roman soldiers carried a large wooden rectangle called a *scutum*. Roman cavalry used a small, round shield, often of leather. The distinctive kite-shaped shield of the Normans became popular in the 12th century and the style endured for 300 years.

In modern times, riot police often use strong plastic shields when confronting disorderly crowds who are throwing rocks or bottles. ■

Shogun

A Japanese term meaning "general who quells the barbarians," the title of shogun was used by the 8th century for military commanders campaigning against invaders.

From 1192–1867, the military ruler of Japan—not the emperor, who was the national figurehead—was known as the shogun. The Japanese emperor reigned as the national sovereign, but the ruling shogun, who inherited his office, was in charge of the government.

In 1867, the emperor became recognized as the supreme ruler of Japan, and the shogun resigned, giving up all his administrative powers to the imperial government. ■

NORMAN SHIELDS Heraldic symbols decorate medieval shields, indicating a man's house or his overlord; the kite-shaped Norman-style Bayeux shield below bears a winged dragon, often a symbol of war. The kite-shaped shield was the favorite of mounted troops from the 11th–13th centuries because its extra length helped protect the body from lance thrusts.

Norman knight of the 12th century, in full-length mail hauberk with kite-shaped shield.

S

SNIPER
Although rifled guns gave armies the ability to use snipers, until the mid-19th century the killing of unsuspecting soldiers from concealed positions was considered against the custom of war. Snipers came into their own during the American Civil War, and have been used in war ever since. The U.S. Marine sergeant below takes aim from concealment, in the tradition of the sniper, who picks off unsuspecting enemy troops and officers at long range. Improved technology such as high-velocity ammunition, powerful scopes, and night-vision goggles make the sniper more deadly than ever.

Siege Warfare

A siege occurs when an attacking force surrounds a fortified enemy and attempts to prevent supplies or reinforcements from getting through.

While the besieging force bombards the defenders with projectiles or tries to break open a gate or defensive works, the defender hopes to endure longer than the attacker. During a long siege, perhaps of months and even years, the besieger often suffers from hunger and the elements just as much as the besieged.

Before **gunpowder** and firearms came into wide use in the 16th century, the defenders of a strong **castle** had a good chance of holding out—even counterattacking and winning a surprise victory. "Siege engines," such as battering rams and storming towers were not always effective, but powerful cannons made most castles indefensible.

Sieges were still conducted in **World War II** (1939–45), as defenders built vast networks

BESIEGED French crusaders defend Ptolemais (Acre), a walled city they have captured, as Muslim warriors try to retake it in 1291.

of trenches, fortifications, and bunkers. From mid-1941 to January 1944, the Russians held their city of Leningrad against Nazi Germany. The city's three million people suffered from starvation, cold, and bombardment, but they held out more than 31 months until the Germans were driven back and the siege was finally broken. ■

Sino-Japanese War

Arising from a long struggle for supremacy on the Korean Peninsula, this conflict from 1894–95 brought victorious Japan to the fore as a new world power.

For hundreds of years, the Chinese Empire dominated Korea, but in the mid-19th century Japan encouraged the Koreans to declare independence from China.

Japan was industrializing and wanted to control Korea's coal and iron mines. The Japanese even encouraged anti-Chinese revolts in Korea.

Hostility flared into open conflict in 1894, when Japan sent 8,000 troops into Korea to support a rebellion, and war was declared. The Chinese army was enormous, but poorly equipped, while the Japanese military had modern weapons, including a powerful new navy.

The Japanese won quick and decisive victories, and by spring 1895 had marched into the Chinese provinces of Manchuria and Shantung.

Treaty terms compelled China to recognize Korean independence and to gave up the island of Taiwan and Manchuria's Liaotung Peninsula to Japan. ■

South American Wars of Independence

In the early 1800s, Spain was involved as an ally of France in the **Napoleonic Wars,** and the Spanish colonies in South America saw their opportunity for winning independence.

Argentine nationalism emerged in 1806–07, when its colonists beat back two attempts by the British to take the colony. From then on, Argentine independence was

never challenged by Spain, whose soldiers were occupied in Europe. Argentina established an independent government in 1816. Other South American colonies began to press for independence under the leadership of **Simón Bolívar**.

Colombia was founded in 1819 out of the colony of New Granada, and two more nations emerged from this same region: Venezuela, 1829, and Ecuador, 1830.

Chile had won independence from Spain by 1821, and Peru by 1824. Brazil became independent of Portugal in 1822. In 1828, Uruguay was the 10th South American country to achieve independence, struggling against both Argentina and Brazil, which tried to control it. ■

Spanish Armada

In May 1588, Spain's King Philip II sent a great fleet of 130 ships, 8,000 sailors, and 19,000 infantry against England and Queen Elizabeth I. The armada—a fleet of armed ships—intended to destroy the English fleet, then pick up a Spanish army on the French coast and transport it to invade England.

Approximately 110 English vessels met the armada off the south coast of England, fighting three engagements from July 31st to August 4. The Spanish wanted to board the enemy ships, but the English kept firing at long range, avoiding close combat. The armada had to sail for Calais and the waiting army.

That army was not ready, however. It was bottled up by England's allies, the Dutch, who had been at war with Spain for generations. The entire campaign was a failure. Now the English fleet had the wind at their backs, preventing the armada from sailing westward and home. There was no choice but to head north around Scotland to get back to Spain.

First, the English attacked, their long-range guns inflicting terrible damage on the Spanish fleet as it struggled to escape. By the time the armada's last ships arrived home in October, after suffering storms and shipwrecks, only 76 vessels remained. ■

Spanish Civil War

This war from 1936–1939 was a testing ground for new military weapons that soon would be employed in **World War II** (1939–45).

Fighting broke out when nationalist generals revolted against the republic.

Supported by Nazi Germany and Fascist Italy, the anti-republican forces

AGAINST THE WIND
The wind favors the English ships, right, as they advance on the Spanish Armada in the English Channel in 1588; several vessels are already engaged in the foreground, but the ships did not often come to grips in this series of battles, which were decided by long-range gunnery.

SPIES, ESPIONAGE

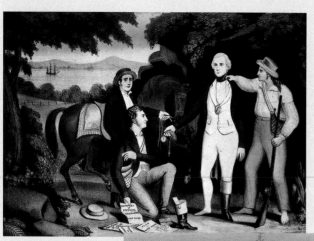

British spy John Andre is captured during the Revolutionary War; he was collaborating with turncoat general Benedict Arnold.

The Predator Unmanned Aerial Vehicle (UAV) sends back real-time infrared and color video to analysts on the ground.

World War II code-breaking machine used to help break the Japanese military code.

Former slave Harriet Tubman provided military intelligence to Union forces operating against Confederates in South Carolina.

Belle Boyd, Civil War espionage agent and secret courier, was a valuable spy for the Confederacy.

Individuals who secretly gather information about the country they live in, and pass it on to another country, are termed spies. The word is derived from "espionage," which spies conduct.

The most valuable spies are in government or military posts where important information is easily available to them. Movies and novels dramatically portray secret agents breaking into safes to steal important plans, or show them hunting other spies and being hunted in turn. Yet most spying is done by simply passing on information that appears on the spy's desk as a routine part of his or her job.

In the 15th century, states began to open embassies in foreign lands, and these became valuable centers for gathering "intelligence." Intelligence and counter-intelligence are the broad terms for espionage, and include the analysis of the information that is gathered. Counter-intelligence is the thwarting and discovery of enemy spies, and breaking secret codes—often using electronic devices and computers for analysis.

Intelligence work involves many thousands of employees in every major country. Vast quantities of information is gathered by office staffs who read foreign newspapers and magazines and closely follow the electronic media. This information is analyzed by experts, and intelligence reports are written.

Throughout history, the spy was always in danger of execution if exposed. Until the 19th century, spies were considered dishonorable because they betrayed the faith of the people with whom they lived. For that reason, most people refused to be spies. After the American Revolution, the key spies who served the patriot cause were never revealed or publicly awarded even though their work was essential to victory.

were led by General Francisco Franco. German "volunteers" for Franco arrived fully equipped, with tanks, artillery, and **anti-aircraft guns**. At least 50,000 Italian and 10,000 German soldiers fought for the anti-republicans. The latest German fighters and bombers perfected methods of carpet-bombing, dive-bombing, and the use of napalm.

Spanish government forces consisted of only 20,000 loyal soldiers and a poorly armed militia, as well as "international brigades" of several thousand volunteers, many of them Communists. Most nations called for non-intervention and provided no military support or arms to the republicans. Spain's gold reserves were spent to buy Russian military equipment, but Franco was simply too powerful, and he took control of the country.

The Spanish Civil War cost 611,000 lives, including 200,000 civilians. ■

Spanish-American War

A brief struggle between the U.S. and Spain in 1898, this "Splendid Little War," as Americans called it, ended four centuries of Spanish colonial rule in the Americas. It also opened an era of American colonialism in the Caribbean and the Pacific.

An insurrection by Cuban revolutionaries against Spanish rule won broad sympathy in the U.S., where business interests saw opportunity in the Caribbean without the presence of Spain. In February 1898, the American **battleship** U.S.S. *Maine* blew up in Havana harbor, killing 260 sailors. No one knew why the ship blew up, but Spain was accused. That April, the U.S. recognized Cuban independence and demanded Spain's withdrawal from the island. Spain broke off diplomatic relations, and the U.S. declared war.

American land and sea power soon won victory, both in the Caribbean and in the Philippines, Spain's East Asian colony, where a Spanish fleet in Manila Bay was defeated in May. Early in July, Americans captured a dug-in Spanish force on San Juan Hill, near Santiago, Cuba. At the same time, the Spanish fleet was destroyed in Santiago harbor.

Hostilities ended in August, with Spain withdrawing from Cuba and ceding the islands of Puerto Rico and Guam to the

ROUGH RIDERS
Gathered around Theodore Roosevelt, their lieutenant-colonel and commander, members of the 1st U.S. Volunteer Cavalry regiment pose for a picture during the Spanish-American War (1898). Nicknamed the "Rough Riders," these cavalrymen took part in the assault against Spanish-held positions at El Caney and San Juan Hill. The regiment was part of an 8,400-man force that attacked and captured San Juan Hill, part of the chain of Spanish defenses around the port city of Santiago. Although they were cavalrymen, the terrain of San Juan Hill forced the Rough Riders to fight on foot.

VICTORY IN CUBA The U.S. Navy resoundingly defeated the Spanish fleet in the Spanish-American War, both in the Philippines and here in Cuban waters, where the triumphant American fleet is seen steaming.

SUBMARINES

U–5 of the German *Kriegsmarine* (navy), around 1910, running on the surface with a large wireless mast for radio communication.

German U-boat (*Unterseeboot*) surfaces to fire its deck gun at an unarmed merchant ship.

The *Seawolf* was the U.S. Navy's newest attack submarine in 1996, equipped with the most advanced quieting technology, weaponry, tactical capability, and communications.

In 1864, the Confederacy's *Hunley* was the first submarine to sink a ship in combat; its victim was the USS *Housatonic,* in Charleston harbor.

The first combat vessel capable of underwater operations was the *Turtle,* invented in 1776 by American patriots during the Revolutionary War (1775–83). The *Turtle* attempted to fix a bomb to a British warship in New York harbor. It failed, but submarine warfare was under way.

As early as 1578, designs show a boat that could be rowed underwater. Many submarine designs were tried over the centuries, but military application was not practical until electric motors were developed just before **World War I** (1914–18). Self-propelled torpedoes were then the most deadly armament of the submarine, although it could surface to fire deck guns at defenseless merchant ships.

After World War I, submarine technology raced ahead. In 1928, the U.S. built the *Argonaut,* the navy's first large, long-range submarine. In the U-boat of **World War II** (1939–45), Germany possessed the most advanced submarine technology. Her ally, Japan, had one-man submarines for sabotage, and also built the largest submarine of the day, capable of carrying three aircraft. By the end of the war, the Allies waged effective anti-submarine warfare, employing aircraft patrols, underwater explosives, and anti-submarine submarines.

By the mid-1950s, submarine technology included nuclear power. With no need to take on fuel, nuclear-powered submarines have an almost unlimited range. In addition to torpedoes, modern submarines carry guided missiles that can be launched from under water at targets thousands of miles away.

In 1997, the Navy's first nuclear-powered attack submarine, USS *Annapolis,* is steered into the Persian Gulf by crewmen who make up the team at the helm or on watch.

U.S. Spain also turned over the Philippines to the U.S. for $20 million.

The war helped make the reputation of American cavalry officer (and later U.S. president) Theodore Roosevelt, who was in the assault on San Juan Hill. ■

Spencer Rifle

An important weapon in the mid-19th century, the Spencer is a "carbine," meaning it has a magazine of cartridges that can be fired without stopping to reload.

The Spencer's magazine holds seven cartridges, which are loaded into the firing chamber by a lever that is part of the trigger guard. The rifle is a breechloader because the cartridges are fed into the firing chamber from the back, or breech, of the weapon.

The Spencer was patented in 1860, but its immense firepower in the hands of soldiers was not recognized until late in the Civil War (1861–65).

Select Union regiments were equipped with Spencer carbines for the last battles of the war. Their firepower was such that Confederate opponents thought the few hundred riflemen they faced actually were many thousands. ■

Spitfire

This famous single-seat British fighter of **World War II** (1939–45) came to symbolize the nation's courageous resistance against the overwhelming military power of Nazi Germany.

After France surrendered in mid-1940, Germany unleashed a massive air war known as the "Battle of Britain." The Germans aimed to destroy Royal Air Force (RAF) planes, terrorize the population, and so prepare the way for an invasion. With superior numbers, especially in their vaunted fighters, the **Messerschmidt 109,** Germany at first launched air raids during the day.

The Spitfire proved a match for the Me109, however, and heavy losses made the Nazis change to night bombing. After a few months, Germany gave up the air campaign. The RAF won the Battle of Britain largely thanks to its fighter pilots and the ground crews who serviced the planes.

More than 20,000 Spitfires were built during the war. A late-model Spitfire had a 2,035hp Rolls-Royce Griffon engine, and had a maximum air speed of 448mph. Armament was two 20mm cannons and two machine guns along with 500 lbs of bombs or rockets. ■

BRITISH SPITFIRES A pilot prepares to start the engine of his Spitfire, Britain's best-known fighter of World War II; the planes are painted with camouflage colors, and they have the circular red, white, and blue insignia of the Royal Air Force.

A SUBMARINE TORPEDO
American crewmen load a Mark 48 "heavyweight" torpedo—one of the 20th-century's largest—into a nuclear-powered attack submarine. Torpedoes are self-propelled, guided projectiles that operate underwater and are designed to detonate when reaching the target. They also can be launched from surface ships, helicopters, and fixed-wing aircraft. The Mark 48 was especially intended for combat against fast, deep-diving enemy submarines and also against "high-performance" surface ships. Torpedos have been used in combat since World War I, and many innovations over time increased their effectiveness. Torpedos can be designed to explode on contact or in proximity to engine noise—and in the case of a magnetic torpedo, by the steel hull of a ship.

T-U

T-34 Russian Tank

This formidable main battle tank of the Russian army during **World War II** (1939–45) was produced in the tens of thousands during the war. Highly mobile and powerfully armed, the T-34 was a match for the best German armor.

The T-34 was the prototype for Soviet tanks in the decades to follow. As would most future tanks, the T-34 had a low profile, helping conceal it and reducing its visibility to the enemy. The T-34 was steadily improved, its cannon increasing in size to 85mm. The T-34 and the German **Tiger tank** shared similar characteristics, with both of them effective at destroying enemy armor from long range.

Later T-34 models were not as heavily armored as many other contemporary tanks of the late 20th century. Instead, they were designed for simplicity of maintenance, speed, and agility over all types of terrain, where they could intimidate opponents of Communist regimes. The T-34 was also designed for swift penetration of enemy lines, following the philosophy that the best defense is a good offense. ∎

Texan War of Independence

Late in 1835, American and Mexican settlers in the Mexican state of Texas began an insurrection to win independence from the central government in Mexico City.

In February 1836, troops led by Mexican president Antonio Lopéz de Santa Anna besieged a force of 200 "Texians"–as the rebels were known–at San Antonio's Alamo mission. The rebels were led by James Bowie and Colonel William B. Travis, who vowed never to surrender. Santa Anna stormed the Alamo on March 6, 1836, and killed all the defenders, executing the few who survived the assault.

"Remember the Alamo!" was the battle cry of Texians who defeated and captured Santa Anna at the Battle of San Jacinto in April 1836. The victory won Texas her independence from Mexico that year. ∎

Thirty Years' War

Actually a 40-year struggle across Europe, the Thirty Years' War (1618–48, 1648–59) was fought mainly in the German states, leaving them destroyed and plundered by the armies battling back and forth.

Until 1637, the war was fought mainly by Catholic Spain and the Holy Roman Empire against Protestant Denmark, Norway, and Sweden. The war was not just

REMEMBER THE ALAMO!
Doomed "Texian" revolutionaries, here led by Davy Crockett (in the coonskin cap), fire at attacking Mexican government troops, who recaptured the makeshift fortress and killed all the defenders.

TANK

Tanks are the modern land army's primary offensive weapon. They are self-propelled armored vehicles, using "caterpillar" tracks, and mounted with cannons and machine guns.

The first tanks appeared in 1916, designed by the British for use against the Germans on the Western Front of **World War I** (1914–18). They were top-secret when shipped to the front, and referred to as "water tanks." The name stuck.

Tanks broke through enemy fortifications and barbed-wire, but they were slow, with a top speed of four mph. Improvements brought lighter, faster tanks into the field and they acquired movable turrets with a cannon. They became known as "armor."

World War II (1939–45) brought the tank into its own. German tanks were organized into **panzer** (armored) divisions with "mechanized" infantry carried in trucks and armored vehicles. In 1940, these divisions raced across northern France in just seven days. German panzer organization, design, and battle techniques were copied by most armies. Tanks became larger, faster, more heavily armored, and had high-velocity cannons.

Late 20th-century warfare saw mighty tank battles, with the largest taking place in the **Arab-Israeli wars** of the 1960s–70s.

Tanks inspired the development of other armored fighting vehicles and self-propelled guns of many types. These include armored amphibious-landing vehicles, Mechanized Infantry Combat Vehicles, and armored "gun-launchers" that fire guided missiles and armor-piercing ammunition.

A British World War I tank demonstrates its ability to cross trenches.

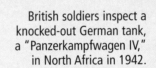

French Renault light tanks on the attack with American troops in France, 1918.

British soldiers inspect a knocked-out German tank, a "Panzerkampfwagen IV," in North Africa in 1942.

M1A1 Abrams tank, armed with a 120mm cannon.

T

ANTI-TANK WEAPON

The earliest anti-tank weapons were high-velocity guns firing hardened ammunition designed to penetrate a tank's armor. The most famous and effective anti-tank gun of World War II was the multi-purpose German 88mm cannon, a gun also used for anti-aircraft defense.

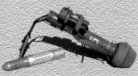

The AT-4 anti-tank weapon is an expendable, self-contained rocket launcher that fires a rocket with a war-head designed to penetrate the armor plate of tanks and armored vehicles.

A U.S. Marine in a reconnaissance force prepares to fire an AT-4 light anti-tank weapon during training exercises. Shoulder-fired, light-weight anti-tank mis-siles make infantry-men extremely dan-gerous to unsuspect-ing crews of armored vehicles.

religious, however, for Catholic France entered on the Protestant side because it was at war with Spain.

The Thirty Years' War brought to fame Sweden's general-king, Gustavus Adolphus, whose tactics and innovative use of horse-drawn artillery completely changed warfare.

Peace treaties in 1648 recognized Switzerland and the United Netherlands republic. A final phase of the war lasted until 1659, mainly fought between France, allied with England, against Spain, which was finally forced to give up her claims to the Netherlands. ■

Tiger Tank

The Tiger tank was designed by Nazi Germany late in **World War II** (1939–45) to match the powerful Russian **T-34** tank.

One model, "King" Tiger, weighed 68 tons and was the heaviest tank used in the war. The King Tiger's primary role was to "kill" enemy tanks. Armed with a long-range 88mm cannon, the King Tiger was heavily armored, designed to resist or deflect the impact of shells.

The Tiger went into action in support of German medium tanks, attempting to destroy opposing tanks before they could bring their own, less-powerful, cannons into range. Fewer than 500 were produced. ■

U.S. Civil War

The Civil War (1861–65) was fought to keep the American union of 44 states together. Those 11 Southern States that seceded between December 1860 and May 1861 called themselves the Confederate States of America.

Confederates claimed the right of states to govern themselves, and they objected to Northern demands for an end to Southern slavery. Unionists took up arms in the belief the union was sacred, but abolition of slavery was not at first a major reason for opposing secession.

After South Carolina secessionists forced

the surrender of the government fort in Charleston harbor in April 1861, U.S. President Abraham Lincoln called for 75,000 volunteers to put down the insurrection. War raged for four years, with the Confederacy successful in the first campaigns, as the Union changed commanders frequently. The main Confederate general was **Robert E. Lee,** whose defeat at Gettysburg, Pennsylvania, in July 1863, put the Confederacy on the defense.

The capture of the Mississippi Valley in this time split the Confederacy in half, further weakening her. Union general **Ulysses S. Grant,** instrumental in the Mississippi campaign, was chosen by Lincoln to lead the North's armies. Grant began a bloody war of attrition against Lee, fighting battle after battle, with no letup. The outnumbered Lee, lacking supplies, surrendered in April 1865, effectively ending the war.

The Union put 1.56 million men under arms, the Confederacy 1.08 million. Union losses were 359,528 dead (110,070 the result of battle wounds) and 275,175 wounded. Confederate losses were approximately 258,000 dead (94,000 from battle) and more than 100,000 wounded. ■

BLOODY ANGLE The 1864 fight for a position termed the "Bloody Angle" was one of the Civil War's most savage struggles.

UNIFORMS

Military dress can be divided into two main categories: parade uniforms and combat uniforms. Modern soldiers look much alike in their fatigues of olive drab and camouflage colors, although parade, or dress, uniforms are usually distinctive from country to country.

Military uniforms came into general use by the late 17th century. Until then, soldiers had ways to recognize comrades in the smoke and fury of battle—perhaps all wearing a plume of a certain color, or with a similar sash over the shoulder, known as "field signs." The wealthy nations of the 18th and 19th centuries garbed their regiments in matching uniforms of bright scarlet, blue, green, and white, with colorful trimmings and distinctive headgear.

While soldiers often wore overalls or working garb when employed around camp or on fortifications, their handsome dress uniforms were usually worn into battle in a spectacular display of pride and glory.

In many armies, each regiment's uniform was different. As a result, soldiers sometimes accidentally fired on their own troops, thinking they were the enemy because of their uniform colors. During the **Napoleonic Wars,** some broad color schemes became recognized, with the British mostly in red coats, the French in blue, Austrians in white, Germans often in green or blue, and the Russians in green.

Uniform colors turned more drab at the opening of the 20th century, as battle formations opened up in the face of immense firepower. The glorious charges of brilliantly uniformed soldiers advancing in ranks gave way to squad tactics, deadly artillery barrages, the machine gun, and combat aircraft.

The modern infantryman fights from behind cover, with his drab uniform's main purpose being to help conceal him from the enemy.

Russian Guards and light infantry of the Napoleonic Wars, in their characteristic green coats, ca. 1803.

U.S. cavalry, infantry, and infantry officer of the Mexican War, 1847.

Bugler's shell jacket, Union cavalry, ca. 1862

A U.S. Marine in full combat gear with an M-60E3 machine gun during 1989 operations in South Korea.

British troops in the American colonies from 1739–43 included Scottish Highlanders, left, and Redcoat grenadiers, right.

Vietnam War

France withdrew from Indochina in 1954, leaving Vietnam, her former colony, divided in two: the Communist Democratic Republic of Vietnam in the North, and the Republic of Vietnam in the South. Elections for reunification were to have been held, but South Vietnam refused.

By 1961, South Vietnamese Communists—mainly the National Liberation Front (NLF)—were waging an armed struggle. The U.S. gave military aid to South Vietnam, and by 1962 had 11,000 soldiers there. The Army of the Republic of Vietnam (ARVN), trained and equipped by the U.S., held the cities, but the Communists controlled the countryside.

The NLF was joined by troops from the North, and Russia and China provided material aid to North Vietnam. In 1965, when the U.S. began bombing the North, more than 184,000 Americans were in action. By 1969, 543,000 Americans were in Vietnam. U.S. troops had great success against the NLF and North Vietnamese regulars, driving them out of areas that once had seemed impregnable. Yet, popular support for the Communists steadily increased.

The war dragged on, until a cease-fire was agreed to in 1973, and U.S. troops were withdrawn. Warfare continued, however, and the Communists took control of Vietnam in April 1975.

The Communist forces lost more than 650,000 killed in action, the ARVN 243,000. The U.S. had more than 58,000 dead from combat and non-combat causes. Half a million Vietnamese civilians were killed, more than a million wounded. ■

War of 1812

As the **Napoleonic Wars** (1803–14) raged on land and sea, the United States found herself caught between the main combatants, Britain and France.

Royal Navy warships pressed American sailors into service, taking men off their vessels on the high seas. Also, the U.S. was subjected to a British blockade that prevented trade with France. On June 18, 1812, President James Madison persuaded Congress to declare war on Britain, which a generation earlier had lost the **American Revolutionary War** (1775–83).

Most battles were fought along the American and Canadian borders and adjacent waterways with mixed results—generally going against the Americans. The British captured and burned Washington, D.C. in 1814. During this campaign, the

A ROYAL WARSHIP DISMASTED
Cannon fire from the U.S. frigate *United States,* right, has snapped the masts of the British vessel, *Macedonian,* which will soon surrender; the engagement took place off the Madiera Islands in the Atlantic.

naval bombardment of Fort McHenry inspired poet Francis Scott Key to write the words to the future national anthem, "The Star-spangled Banner."

The war's greatest battle was fought at New Orleans on January 8, 1815, several days after peace terms had been signed in Ghent, Belgium. The British frontal assault on General Andrew Jackson's fortified lines cost the British more than 2,000 casualties, including the British commander and two other generals. The Americans lost eight dead and 13 wounded. ■

War of the Austrian Succession

The right of Austria's princess Maria Theresa to inherit the throne of the Holy Roman Empire was challenged by several European rulers who wanted the crown. In addition, Prussian king **Frederick the Great** seized the Austrian province of Silesia in 1740.

Prussia found allies in France, Spain, and Bavaria, to oppose Austria, Britain, the Netherlands, and Sardinia. Russia joined Austria in 1746. In North America, the conflict was known as **King George's War**. Italy and India also became battlegrounds.

By the end of the war in 1748, Maria Theresa retained her rulership, although her husband, Francis I, was officially named emperor, and Prussia kept Silesia. ■

War of the Spanish Succession

Upon the death of the childless Spanish king, Charles II, in 1700, King Louis XIV of France declared his own grandson, Philip, duke of Anjou, would take the Spanish throne. War officially began the next year.

In opposition, a "Grand Alliance" of Britain, the Netherlands, and the Holy Roman Empire declared war on France early in 1702. Prussia soon joined the alliance, and Portugal and Sardinia came and went and also changed sides. In North America, the fighting was named **Queen Anne's War,** after the English monarch.

Peace treaties in 1713–14 recognized Philip as king of Spain, but gave control of the Spanish Netherlands (Belgium) to Austria. ■

War on Terrorism

This campaign to destroy terrorist networks around the world came in response to the hijacking of four commercial airliners in

LOUIS XIV (1638–1715)
France's King Louis XIV was a strong ruler, who was also a masterful military organizer and leader, extending his nation's borders and influence. A champion of French culture and famous for his pomp and lavish style, Louis, also called the "Sun King," is considered the greatest monarch of his era. His armies, however, brought the horrors of war to many neighboring lands, and he was at war for most of his long reign. At his high point, Louis overcame powerful coalitions of nations, but he also made many enemies. In the War of the Spanish Succession (1701–14), he lost much of what he had gained by a lifetime of war and diplomacy, but French borders were kept intact.

U.S. ARMOR IN AFGHANISTAN Marines in LAV armored personnel carriers search for Al Qaeda terrorists near Kandahar, Afghanistan, during the 2002 campaign known as Operation Enduring Freedom.

W

AFGHAN FIGHTER
An Anti-Taliban Forces (ATF) soldier wraps a bandoleer of ammunition around his body while participating with U.S. Marines in a raid against suspected terrorist positions in Afghanistan in 2002. Native Afghan fighters who opposed the strict fundamentalist rule of the Taliban party took advantage of a U.S. bombing campaign to launch attacks that drove the Taliban from power. With the Taliban went their allies in the Muslim terrorist organization known as Al Qaeda.

the U.S. on September 11, 2001. Two airliners were flown into New York City's World Trade Center, destroying it, and a third struck the Pentagon in northern Virginia. The fourth plane crashed in a Pennsylvania field after the passengers resisted the hijackers.

Almost 3,000 persons, most of them Americans, were killed in this attack on the U.S., which was carried out by Muslim radicals.

In an effort led by the U.S., scores of nations around the world cooperated in seeking out terrorist organizations and also in blocking financial accounts believed to be aiding them. Further, an international coalition took action against countries that harbored terrorist organizations.

Soon after the attack on the U.S., the coalition undertook its first military operation, moving against Afghanistan. There, the ruling Taliban party—Muslim fundamentalists—had allied itself with accused terrorist leader Osama bin Laden, a wealthy Saudi living in Afghanistan. Bin Laden was considered the mastermind and financial backer of the suicide missions on September 11th. He was a leader of a secret Muslim terrorist organization known as Al Qaeda, meaning "the base."

In the Afghanistan military campaign of 2001–02, the international coalition supplied an alliance of Afghani opposition forces that had been fighting the Taliban for several years. The alliance was supported on the ground by American Special Forces while coalition warplanes struck military targets controlled by the Taliban. The anti-Taliban alliance, aided by the bombing campaign and the Special Forces, quickly drove the Taliban from power, and Bin Laden disappeared.

The subsequent hunt for Bin Laden and Al Qaeda members was part of a worldwide "War on Terrorism," which focused on radical cells that are scattered from Indonesia to Chechnya and Western Europe, from the Middle East to the U.S. and South America. ∎

Washington, George (1732–99)

As commander in chief of the American army during the **American Revolutionary War** (1775–83), George Washington faced daunting odds against the British military, the most powerful in the world.

A Virginia native, Washington had commanded troops in the **French and Indian War** (1755–63). At the outbreak of the Revolution in mid-1775, he hurried to Boston to take charge of the patriot militia besieging British troops in the city. He also organized other campaigns, built an officer corps, and enforced discipline on the unruly militia. Early in 1776, Washington placed cannons overlooking Boston, and the British sailed away.

The rest of that year was disastrous. The British defeated Washington on Long Island, captured New York City, and drove him back to Pennsylvania. That winter, he counterattacked in New Jersey, defeating the king's troops at Trenton and Princeton.

Although Washington was defeated in 1777 at Brandywine and Germantown, losing

GENERAL WASHINGTON This portrait honors George Washington's triumph at Princeton in the American Revolutionary War.

Naval power was essential to the rise of early empires, both to dominate the movements of trading vessels or to capture and plunder them.

Controlling sea trade or protecting one's own traders from enemy ships were basic military tasks as long ago as Egyptian and Babylonian times. The naval might of Athens and Persia in the 5th century BC won them great empires, but also brought on war between them for rulership of the seas.

The rakish, swift row-galleys of Greek and Roman eras approached a sea battle as if they were armies on land. Vessels were grouped into divisions that attempted to trap smaller groups of enemy ships. Bows rammed the sides of the opponent's vessel, lines and hooks were thrown to pull ships together, and warriors leaped across to join battle.

By the 15th century, sea engagements were dominated by artillery duels more than close fighting. After the defeat of the **Spanish Armada** by the English in the 16th century, long-range artillery was favored. For another 200 years, sailing ships maneuvered for a favorable wind and stood off at a distance, battering each other with cannon balls.

In the 19th century, steam power made it possible for a vessel to move without the wind. Warships were armored with iron, then steel, and were designed in all sizes and shapes: heavily armed **battleships**; medium-sized cruisers; smaller destroyers, and fast **coast guard** patrol boats. Submarines and **aircraft carriers** appeared in the 20th century, and were even more effective than huge battleships, which were almost helpless against air attack or a submarine's torpedoes.

The image of a Roman war vessel with a ram at the prow is carved in stone.

In 1340, the English fleet destroyed the French in the Battle of Sluys, a Hundred Years' War engagement in the Lowlands.

This 1770s Royal Navy warship with 90 guns was one of the most powerful vessels in the British fleet.

The 19th-century Chinese junk of war was designed to ply the many narrow straits and shallow waters of the East Asian coastline.

The U.S. steel warship, *Oregon*, races toward action in Cuban waters during the Spanish-American War.

The U.S. cruiser *Port Royal,* equipped with Tomahawk anti-ship and land-attack missiles, steams through the Persian Gulf in 1997.

W

Philadelphia, he kept his army together. The next summer, he forced the British to abandon Philadelphia, and engaged them in a hard-fought draw at Monmouth, New Jersey. Washington's greatest triumph, won in alliance with the French army and navy at Yorktown in 1781, signaled the final defeat of the British. Still, he had to keep his army in readiness for two more years, until peace terms were finalized late in 1783.

Washington went on to become the first U.S. president. ■

Wellington, Duke of (1769–1852)

British general Sir Arthur Wellesley first won his military reputation in the 1808–14 Peninsular War—in Spain and Portugal—fighting against the occupying forces of France, led by **Napoleon Bonaparte**.

Wellesley's victories encouraged other European nations to oppose Napoleon, who was beaten in April 1814. Wellesley was rewarded with the title Duke of Wellington.

When Napoleon returned from exile the following March, Wellington assumed command of the British and allied armies that joined the Prussians for the Waterloo campaign. Napoleon lost at Waterloo on June 18th, and Wellington earned most of the credit for the triumph.

Wellington was against punishing France vindictively. He used his influence as a popular British hero to organize financial support for the defeated nation. Later he worked to relieve the oppression of Catholics in Ireland, where his family held its estate. He went on to become British prime minister in the Tory party.

Throughout his long career, Wellington did what he thought best for his country, though this often brought him harsh political criticism. As an officer, he enforced strict discipline that earned him the posthumous title, "Iron Duke," but in private life he was modest and reserved. Wellington's favorite saying was, "I am but a man." ■

World War I

Known as the "War to end all wars," this global struggle from 1914–18 cost the lives of more than ten million soldiers.

Also called the "Great War," it was sparked by a dispute in the Balkans, where the Austro-Hungarian empire was losing influence over its former states. The assassination of an Austro-Hungarian prince by a Serbian nationalist at Sarajevo in June 1914 set in motion a chain of events that led to war.

Russia supported Serbia and was joined by France (the Allies). Austria-Hungary allied with Germany and Turkey (the Central Powers). When Germany attacked France through Belgium in August 1914, Britain declared war on Germany. Italy joined the Allies in 1915.

Trenches soon lined hundreds of miles of the stalemated "Western Front" in France and Belgium. In the East, the Russians were outfought by the Central Powers, but the battles were indecisive. Then Russia collapsed under the stress of internal revolution as the Communists overthrew the

OVER THE TOP
Knowing they one day will be met by a deadly hail of enemy bullets, Canadian infantrymen in World War I train to go "over the top," as charging out of the trenches was called; they are near St. Pol, France, in 1916.

WOMEN AT WAR

Women have played a vital part in every war, at first as supporters of the soldiers, tending their wounds, and following the armies on campaigns. It was for the women, often relatives of the soldiers, to be there at the close of battle to help the wounded and support what few doctors and surgeons were available.

The situation changed for the better in the mid-19th century, when courageous nurses—Clara Barton in the United States and Florence Nightingale in Britain—challenged the military establishment and demanded hygienic hospital wards and sanitary conditions for the troops. They proved that a healthy army is a more effective army.

In wartime, women often risked their lives as spies or as couriers passing on messages. Many wars have stories of women who crossed enemy lines undisturbed while bearing important information that changed the course of a conflict. In the **American Revolutionary War** (1775–83), **George Washington** often depended on patriot courier Deborah Champion, who rode back and forth 75 miles to his headquarters with dispatches from her father, an American general.

In modern armies, women are crucial in administrative and technical positions. They also have assumed combat roles, including training with infantry weapons. In the American air force, women are accomplished pilots; the army had its first woman general, and in the navy women command warships.

Nurse Florence Nightingale goes the nightly rounds, tending British wounded in the Crimean War.

The visionary Joan of Arc led French soldiers to victories in the 1400s.

With many men in military service, women worked in the war industry, as did these World War I ship-construction employees at the Seattle Navy Yard.

French *cantiniére,* ca. 1865—brandy was carried in the keg at her side. These women were officially attached to regiments to provide brandy to the soldiers.

An American Red Cross nurse of World War I.

The first woman Marine selected for flight duty, Lieutenant Keri Lynn Schubert prepares to pilot her Hornet fighter jet.

W

THE BOAT THAT WON THE WAR
Landing craft were key to the success of the Allied counter invasions of enemy-held territory in World War II. General Eisenhower praised designer and builder Andrew Higgins as "the man who won the war for us." The "Higgins Boats"—infantry landing craft (LCVP's) and others that landed vehicles and equipment—allowed the U.S. and its allies to land combat forces over open beaches. Often coming in under heavy enemy fire, landing craft pushed into shore, dropped their ramps, and unloaded their troops and equipment. Pictured are American soldiers charging ashore through waist-deep waters. Assaults against German and Italian forces in Europe and against Japanese-occupied islands in the Pacific theater depended on landing craft.

czar in 1917. The U.S. entered the war in April that year, mainly in response to German submarines sinking American ships.

Fresh U.S. forces tipped the balance in favor of the Allies, who launched a sustained offensive against Germany in mid-1918. An armistice was called in November. Subsequent peace terms in the Treaty of Versailles divided up the Central Powers into several smaller nations.

Military technology advanced during World War I, with airplanes, tanks, submarines, and radio communications developing swiftly. Machine guns and artillery became more destructive than anyone imagined possible. Another result of the war was the rise of intense nationalism and Communism, both of which became new causes for another conflict. A second world war was in the making. ∎

World War II

German bitterness at defeat in **World War I** allowed the rise of Nazism, a nationalistic movement that believed in the superiority of a German race. The Nazis were led by dictator Adolph Hitler, who prepared Germany for war. Hitler was determined to destroy Communism and to wipe out peoples he considered unworthy, such as Jews and Gypsies.

When Hitler's troops invaded Poland in September 1939, Britain and France declared war on Germany. In May 1940, Germany struck through France and the Low Countries, winning a swift victory and occupying the region. Only Britain remained defiant. Italy and several smaller nations joined Germany as the Axis forces, and Britain received material support from the U.S., which was not yet a participant.

In the Far East, Japan was winning a war with China. In June 1941, Germany invaded Russia, and in December Japan attacked the American naval base at Pearl Harbor, Hawaii. Japan joined the Axis powers, and the U.S., Russia, and Britain and its Commonwealth were the Allies. Immense U.S. military production was key to the Allied war effort.

The Americans won a great naval triumph over Japan in the Battle of Midway in June 1942, and Japan was forced onto the defensive. The German invasion of Russia was defeated at Stalingrad late that year. In 1943, the Axis powers had a series of reverses, from North Africa to Italy, which stopped their advance.

On June 6, 1944, the Allies invaded Normandy, part of German-occupied France, and began the final push to defeat the Axis, now overwhelmed from East and West. Hitler committed suicide. Germany gave up on May 8, 1945. In August 1945, two

SOON AFTER D-DAY A few days after the June 6, 1944, invasion called D-Day, reinforcements of men and equipment arrive on "Omaha Beach," as this strip of French coastline was code-named by the Allies.

atomic bombs were dropped on Japanese cities, causing immense death and destruction and forcing Japan's surrender.

The war cost 15 million military dead and missing, and approximately the same number of civilians died in the fighting or were murdered by the Nazi persecutions. ∎

Yugoslavian Wars

After the fall of European Communism in 1989, the Socialist Federal Republic of Yugoslavia also began to fall apart. The various Yugoslavian states were populated by Serbs, Croats, Slovenes, Albanians, and Macedonians, each ethnic group demanding its own territory.

In 1991 Slovenia and Croatia seceded and successfully defended themselves against Yugoslavian troops who tried to overthrow them. Macedonia also declared independence, but was not attacked. In 1992, the mainly Muslim state of Bosnia and Herzegovina declared its independence, but its Serb and Croat minorities objected. Dissident republics of Croats and Serbs were founded, one supported by Croatia and the other by Serbia, the largest Yugoslavian state.

Conflict erupted in Bosnia. Many atrocities were committed against Bosnian Muslims, who suffered "ethnic cleansing," which means eliminating one group from land claimed by another. Serb fighters placed the Bosnian capital of Sarajevo under siege, bombarding the city without mercy. In 1995, the North Atlantic Treaty Organization (NATO) finally arranged an end to the conflict, stationing peacekeeping soldiers in the region.

After the Bosnian struggle, Yugoslavia was only Serbia, Montenegro, and Kosovo.

In 1998, the Serb military oppressed Albanians in Kosovo, and a year later NATO intervened. NATO launched 78 days of air strikes against Yugoslavia until Serb troops finally withdrew from Kosovo, which was occupied by NATO forces and administered by the United Nations. ∎

Zulu-British War

Around the 1820s, the Zulus established themselves as the mightiest native fighting force in southern Africa. Zulu impis—regiments—swept across the region, destroying other native peoples or incorporating them into the Zulu nation.

White farmers called Boers went to war several times with Zulus, but reached peace terms that left Zululand independent. The British Empire took over Boer territory in 1877 and ordered the nearby Zulus to disband their own standing army of many thousand warriors. The Zulus refused, and the British invaded.

In January 1879, an imperial army of 1,800 was wiped out by 20,000 Zulus at Isandhlwana. Another British invasion force followed, this one numbering 5,000 troops. In July, it destroyed the Zulu army, killing 1,500 natives and breaking the nation's power. Zululand then was divided up among South African provinces, which eventually became the Union of South Africa. ∎

WRECKAGE OF DEFEAT
In 1879, British and colonial troops view the remains of an imperial force of 1,800 men wiped out by Zulus at the Battle of Isandhlwana, in southeast Africa. The clash was named for the rock outcrop in the rear, which Zulus call Isandhlwana, roughly meaning "the stomach of an ox."

DICTIONARY OF MILITARY LEADERS

Akbar (1542–1605)
The greatest Mogul emperor of India, he extended Mogul power throughout the Indian subcontinent; he won the support of both Muslim and Hindu populations and created a centralized government.

Ataturk, Kemal (1881–1938)
Founder and first president of the Republic of Turkey; as a field commander during World War I (1914–18) he led the fight against invading Australians and New Zealanders in the 1915–16 Turkish triumph at Gallipoli.

Attila "The Hun" (5th century AD)
King of the nomadic Huns of Central Asia, and one of Rome's greatest adversaries; he attacked Rome's cities in southeastern Europe in 441 and 447, invaded Gaul in 451, and Italy in 452.

Blucher, G.L. (1742–1819)
Prussian field marshal in the Napoleonic Wars (1803–1815); came out of retirement in 1813 to help capture Paris in 1814, and in 1815 reinforced the Allies at Waterloo, completing Napoleon's defeat.

Charles XII of Sweden (1682–1718)
A general-king who led his country during much of the Great Northern War (1700–21), fighting several nations, including Russia, Denmark, Poland, and Saxony; killed while invading Norway.

Charles Louis, Prince of Austria (1771–1847)
Modernizer of the Austrian army, he was one of the few Allied leaders capable of defeating French generals in the wars between 1792–1815; in 1809, he defeated Napoleon at Aspern-Essling, but lost at Wagram.

Ch'ien-lung (1711–99)
Chinese emperor of the Manchu dynasty, whose reign was one of the longest and most successful, enlarging his empire; he defeated Turks and Mongols in the Northwest and established firm control of the Southeast.

Clive, Robert (1725–74)
Established British rule in India while serving the British East India Company; he defeated the French as well as Indian forces, and was twice governor of Bengal.

Condé, the Great (1621–86)
One of French King Louis XIV's best generals, this prince won key victories in the Thirty Years' War (1618–48), then led an unsuccessful uprising of aristocrats. Exiled for years, he returned to military command with continued success.

Cornwallis, Charles (1738–1805)
The most capable British general of the Revolutionary War (1775–83), he won a number of victories over patriot forces; his defeat at Yorktown, Virginia, in 1781, marked the end of British military hopes in America.

Cortéz, Hernan (1485–1547)
Spanish conquistador who conquered Mexico's enormous Aztec empire in 1621; poor health from campaigning and the effects of hostile political intrigues left him a broken man.

Crazy Horse (1842–77)
Oglala Sioux war chief and one of the finest native leaders in the late 19th-century American Indian Wars; he refused to accept the reservation system and led in the 1876 crushing defeat of Custer's 7th Cavalry at the Battle of Little Big Horn.

Cromwell, Oliver (1599–1658)
Puritan soldier and statesman, leader of Parliament's forces in the English Civil War (1642-51); defeated royalist forces and became lord protector, ruler of the British Isles.

Daun, Leopold von (1705–66)
One of Austria's finest field marshals and military reformers, commanded his country's armies against Prussia in the Seven Years' War (1756-63), winning several victories over Frederick the Great.

Hernan Cortéz

Charles Cornwallis

Oliver Cromwell

Doria, Andrea (1466–1560)

Genoese statesman, commander of mercenaries, and admiral, considered the leading naval commander of the time; served various Italian houses, France, and the Vatican, and variously fought the French, Turks, and the Barbary pirates.

Drake, Francis (1540–96)

The most famous English seaman of the Elizabethan age, he sailed around the world between 1577–80; a leading commander in the English 1588 defeat of the Spanish Armada.

Edward, "The Black Prince" (1330–76)

One of the best military leaders of the Hundred Years' War (1337–1453); he led the English to victory at Poitiers in 1356, capturing the French king John II, crippling France's ability to fend off English invaders.

Eugene, Prince (1663–1736)

Austrian general and leading strategist of the day, his theories influenced such military leaders as Frederick the Great and Napoleon; Prince Eugene's victories kept the Ottoman Turks from capturing Hungary. He won the battle of Blenheim with the Duke of Marlborough in 1704 over the French and Bavarians.

Foch, Ferdinand (1851–1929)

French marshal, commander of Allied forces at the close of World War I (1914–18), and credited as the individual most responsible for victory; held his armies together against German assaults in 1918, until American reinforcements arrived.

Franco, Francisco (1892–1975)

Spanish dictator who came to power after leading nationalist forces in the Spanish Civil War (1936–39), overthrowing a democratic government and establishing a Fascist regime.

Giap, Vo Nguyen (1912–)

Chief organizer of the Communist Vietnamese forces that fought Japan, France, and the U.S.; coordinated guerrilla fighting behind enemy lines and was North Vietnam's chief of staff and minister of defense.

Greene, Nathanael (1742–86)

The Revolutionary War's most able strategist after George Washington, who counted on him more than any other commander; he battled Charles Cornwallis, who in 1781 moved to Yorktown, Virginia, and was defeated by Washington and the French.

Gustavus Adolphus (1594–1632)

Sweden's greatest general king, who made his country a leading military power in the Thirty Years' War (1618–48); he developed innovative infantry and artillery tactics which were copied by other armies of the period.

Henry V (1387–1422)

English king who defeated the French at the 1415 Battle of Agincourt in the Hundred Years' War (1337–1453); made England Europe's strongest kingdom and claimed the French throne. He died while on campaign, of fever.

Hindenburg, Paul von (1847–1934)

Prussian-born German field marshal who rose to command all German land forces during World War I (1914–18) and was widely admired by his country despite ultimate defeat. Worked closely with General Ludendorff.

Joan of Arc, Saint (1412–31)

Visionary daughter of a French farmer, she became her country's greatest national hero, leading resistance to the English and Burgundians during the Hundred Years' War (1337–1453); condemned by the church as a heretic and burned at the stake.

Kutuzov, Mikhail (1745–1813)

Marshal of Russian forces who opposed Napoleon's invasion in 1812; withdrew from the field after Battle of Borodino, but kept the army intact. Kutuzov's army harried Napoleon's retreat from Russia.

Ludendorff, Erich (1865–1937)

Staff officer who helped guide the German military during World War I (1914–18); he developed the theory of "total war," meaning that not only soldiers must fight, but whole nations, their economies and politicians, must make war.

MacArthur, Douglas (1880–1964)

Supreme Allied Commander in the Southwest Pacific during World War II (1939-45), who led in the defeat of Japan; MacArthur commanded United Nations forces in the the Korean War (1950-53), but when he urged directly attacking China—which aided the North Koreans—he was dismissed.

Manstein, Erich von (1887–1973)

German field marshal who planned the surprise 1940 panzer invasion through the Ardennes Forest that captured France and the Lowlands during World War II (1939-45).

Francis Drake

Nathanael Greene

Gustavus Adolphus

Douglas MacArthur

Horatio Nelson

George S. Patton

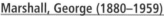

Rameses II

Erwin Rommel

Mao Ze-Dong (1893–1976)
Chinese commander, guerrilla leader, and statesman, who led the Communist revolution that triumphed in 1949; his forces fought both Japanese invaders and Chinese nationalists.

Marshall, George (1880–1959)
U.S. World War II (1939–45) chief of staff; held to the strategy of attacking Germany through France; after the war, as secretary of state, promoted "Marshall Plan" that rebuilt Europe.

Moltke, Helmuth von (1800–91)
Military leader whose reforms as chief of the Prussian and German general staffs helped bring victories against Denmark, Austria, and France and opened the way for German unification as an empire.

Montgomery, Bernard (1887–1976)
British field marshal in World War II, he defeated the Germans in North Africa and later held command positions in the Italian campaign, the invasion of Normandy, and the Allied victory in Europe in 1944–45.

Nelson, Horatio (1758–1805)
Britain's most popular war hero, he commanded fleets in the wars against Revolutionary and Napoleonic France and won great victories; killed in the supreme triumph at Trafalgar.

Nimitz, Chester (1885–1966)
As U.S. admiral in World War II (1939–45), he won a crucial victory over the Japanese fleet at Midway in 1942, and another victory in 1944 at Leyte Gulf, which established decisive American naval superiority in the Pacific.

Parma (Alessandro Farnese), Duke of (1545–92)
Spain's best commander in the rebellious Netherlands; a successful military leader and diplomat, who consolidated the Catholic regions of the Lowlands under Spanish control.

Patton, George S. (1885–1945)
U.S. World War II (1939–45) general whose aggressive, fast-moving thrusts with armored units and motorized infantry won him fame as a top tactical commander in the European campaigns.

Pershing, John J. (1860–1948)
Commander of the U.S. expeditionary force to Europe in World War I (1914–18); after three years of trench warfare, the combatants were exhausted, and Pershing's reinforcements turned the tide in favor of the Allies.

Radetzky, Josef (1766–1858)
Austrian general and national hero, admired by his troops and respected for courage in battle; as Austria's chief of staff, he was a key strategist in the 1813 defeat of Napoleon at Leipzig.

Ramses II, the Great (1304–1237BC)
Egyptian king who battled the Hittite empire and nations of northern Africa; the Egyptian-Hittite conflict is one of the first known wars. The reign of Ramses II was the second-longest in Egyptian history.

Richard I, the "Lion-heart" (1157–99)
English king who spent most of his reign participating in warfare, mainly as a crusader in the Holy Land; the French named him "lion-heart" because of his courage.

Robert I, the Bruce (1274–1329)
King and legendary hero of Scotland who liberated the country from English rule and reestablished the Scottish monarchy; his most famous victory was in 1314 at Bannockburn, the greatest one-day loss of English knights.

Rochambeau, Comte de (1725–1807)
Commander of French forces allied with Americans during the Revolutionary War; helped George Washington plan the victorious 1781 Yorktown campaign.

Rommel, Erwin (1891–1944)
Field marshal of Nazi Germany in World War II (1939–45), known as the "Desert Fox" for his skill in the North African campaigns; implicated in the conspiracy to assassinate Adolf Hitler, he committed suicide to protect his family from Nazi reprisals.

Santa Anna, Antonio Lopéz de (1794–1876)
Mexican leader who helped win independence from Spain in 1829; he became president, and in 1836 was defeated by rebellious Texans. Ten years later, he lost to the U.S. in the Mexican War (1846–48).

Saxe, Herman-Maurice, Comte de (1696–1750)
French field marshal who led King Louis XV's armies during the War of the Austrian Succession (1740–48); a military theorist who wrote influentially on the science of warfare.

Scipio Africanus (236–184BC)
Roman consul who conquered the Carthaginians in Spain and North Africa, defeating their greatest general, Hannibal, at the 202BC Battle of Zama.

Scott, Winfield (1786–1866)
U.S. general in three wars—War of 1812, Mexican War (1846–48), and the Civil War 1861–65); at the start of the Civil War, Scott spurned his native Virginia, which seceded, and remained in command of the U.S. army.

Schwarzkopf, Norman (1934–)
Commander of the operations "Desert Shield" and "Desert Storm" against Iraq in the Gulf War 1991); coordinated Allied campaign to drive Iraq's invading forces out of Kuwait.

Shaka Zulu (1787–1828)
Founder of the Zulu nation of southeastern Africa, he trained a mighty army that devastated a huge region; developed a short stabbing spear—an "assegai"—for close-quarters fighting.

Sherman, William T. (1820–91)
A leading Union general in the Civil War (1861–65), he conducted devastating campaigns into the heart of the Confederacy, bringing about its collapse.

Sitting Bull (1831–90)
Medicine man and chief of the Dakota tribes and leader of the Sioux nation in their wars with the U.S. army; he helped lead the tribes that triumphed at the 1876 Battle of the Little Big Horn.

Stalin, Joseph (1879–1953)
U.S.S.R. Communist dictator who forged his country into a world power; as supreme commander of Soviet forces in World War II (1939–45), he directed the defeat of Nazi German invaders then took control of eastern Europe.

Suleyman I "the Magnificent" (1494–1566)
Sultan of the Ottoman Turkish empire who expanded his rule northward to Hungary and into Persia; he conquered Tripoli in North Africa and made the Ottomans the strongest power in the Mediterranean.

Tamerlane (1336–1405)
Muslim Turkic leader, also known as Timur, who conquered great regions of Central Asia and the Middle East, from Mongolia to the Mediterranean.

Tojo, Hideki (1884–1948)
Japanese prime minister and minister of war during World War II (1939–41), mastermind of Japan's war effort; afterward executed for war crimes.

Turenne, Henri de (1611–75)
Marshal of France in the Thirty Years' War (1618–48), defender of the monarchy in civil war, and famous for his bold and brilliant strategy in later wars of the 1600s.

Vauban, Sebastien (1633–1707)
French military engineer and marshal, the most influential expert in the art of fortification until the mid-19th century; his writings on the construction, attack, and defense of fortifications were studied by engineers in all countries.

Vercingetorix (d. 46BC)
Gallic tribal chieftain and war leader who led a rebellion against the Romans in 52BC; Julius Caesar besieged his army and forced its surrender. Vercingetorix was executed.

Wallenstein, Albrecht von (1583–1634)
Bohemian-born soldier and statesman who won fame as commander of the armies of the Holy Roman Empire during the Thirty Years' War (1618–48); conspiring to benefit himself, he fell out of favor with the emperor and was murdered by imperial mercenaries.

Westmoreland, William (1914–)
From 1964–68, chief commander of the U.S. forces in the Vietnam War (1960–75); unsuccessfully waged a "war of attrition" to wear down the enemy, but failed to weaken their resolve to fight. American chief of staff from 1968–72.

William I, "the Silent" (1533–84)
Leader of Protestants in the Netherlands who revolted against the rule of Catholic Spain; worked to create a united and free Netherlands until he was assassinated by the Spanish.

William I, the Conqueror (1028–87)
As Duke of Normandy, William invaded Saxon-dominated England in 1066, won the Battle of Hastings, and took the English throne.

Xerxes I (519–465BC)
Persian king who continued the attempts of his father, Darius I, to conquer Greece; his forces lost at Marathon in 490BC and again in the great sea battle of Salamis in 480BC.

Yamamoto, Isoroku (1884–1943)
Japanese admiral who planned and led the December 7, 1941, attack on Pearl Harbor, Hawaii, bringing America into World War II (1939–45); killed when his plane was shot down during an inspection tour.

William T. Sherman

Sitting Bull

Vercingetorix

William Westmoreland

RESOURCE GUIDE AND BIBLIOGRAPHY

SELECTED WEBSITES FOR MILITARY HISTORY RESEARCH:

The Airforce Historical Research Agency
http://www.au.af.mil/au/afhra/

American History Archive Project:
Columbia University
http://www.ilt.columbia.edu/
k12/history/aha.html

American Memory: Historical Collections
for the National Digital Library
http://memory.loc.gov/ammem/
amhome.html

The Anne S. K. Brown Military Collection,
Brown University
http://www.brown.edu/Facilities/
University_Library/collections/askb/

The California Military Museum
http://militarymuseum.org/

Canadian War Museum
http://www.civilization.ca/cwm/cwme.asp

DefenseLink (U.S. Department of Defense)
http://www.defenselink.mil/

Frontier Army Museum at Fort
Leavenworth, Kansas
http://leav-www.army.mil/museum/

George Washington Papers at the
Library of Congress
http://lcweb2.loc.gov/ammem/gwhtml/
gwhome.html

Higgins Armory Museum
http://www.higgins.org/

History Net, The
http://history.about.com/

Imperial War Museum
http://www.iwm.org.uk/

Jane's Information Group
(private publication which tracks
military technology)
http://www.janes.com/

The Library of Congress
http://www.loc.gov/

Liddell Hart Centre for Military Archives:
King's College, London
http://www.kcl.ac.uk/lhcma/home.htm

Military History Encyclopedia on the Web
http://www.rickard.karoo.net/
peopleframe.html

National Aeronautics and Space
Administration History Office
http://www.hq.nasa.gov/office/pao/
History/index.html

The National Archives and Records
Administration
http://www.nara.gov/

National Army Museum
http://www.national-army-
museum.ac.uk/

National Museum of Health and Medicine
http://www.natmedmuse.afip.org/

The National Parks Service
http://www.nps.gov/

National War Museum of Scotland
http://www.nms.ac.uk/

Naval Historical Center
http://www.history.navy.mil/

Patton Museum of Cavalry and Armor,
Fort Knox
http://knox-www.army.mil/museum/

Redstone Arsenal Historical Information
http://www.redstone.army.mil/history/

Rutgers Oral History Archives of
World War II
http://fas-history.rutgers.edu/
oralhistory/orlhom.htm

University of Kansas
http://www.ukans.edu/history/VL/
topical/military.html

U.S. Army Center of Military History
http://www.army.mil/cmh-pg/

U.S. Army Engineer Museum
http://www.wood.army.mil/MUSEUM/
mus_info.htm

U.S. Army information and archives
U.S. Army Military History Institute
http://carlisle-www.army.mil/usamhi/

U.S. Army Signal Corps Museum
http://www.gordon.army.mil/museum/

U.S. Civil War Center:
Louisiana State University
http://www.cwc.lsu.edu/

U.S. Military Academy at West Point
http://www.usma.edu/

Virginia Historical Society
http://www.vahistorical.org/

World War I
The Great War: University of Pittsburgh
http://www.pitt.edu/~pugachev/
greatwar/ww1.html

The World War I Document Archive
http://www.lib.byu.edu/~rdh/wwi/

World War II resources
http://www.ibiblio.org/pha/

SUGGESTED READING

Brownstone, David, and Irene Franck.
*Timelines of War: Chronology of
Warfare from 100,000BC to the
Present.* Boston: Little, Brown and
Company, 1994.

Byam, Michele. *Arms and Armor.* New
York: Dorling Kindersley, 1988.

Editors. *Modern Warfare* (Series).
Alexandria, Virginia: Time-Life Books,
1990.

Eggenberger, David. *An Encyclopedia of
Battles.* New York: Dover Publications,
1985.

Frankland, Noble, ed. *The Encyclopedia of
Twentieth Century Warfare.* New York:
Crown Publishers, 1989

Heller, Jonathan (editor). *War & Conflict:
Selected Images from the National
Archives, 1765–1970.* National
Archives and Records Administration,
Washington, D.C. 1990.

Kuehne, Richard E. and McAfee, Michael
J. *The West Point Museum—A Guide
to the Collections.* West Point, New
York: U.S. Military Academy,
Association of Graduates, the Class of
1932, 1987.

Parker, Geoffrey, ed. *Warfare: Cambridge
Illustrated History.* Cambridge:
Cambridge University Press, 1995.

Tarassuk, Leonid, and Claude Blair, eds.
*The Complete Encyclopedia of Arms
and Weapons.* New York: Bonanza
Books, 1986.

Tunis, Edwin. *Weapons—A Pictorial
History.* New York: World Publishing,
1972.

INDEX

ACKNOWLEDGMENTS

Special thanks to: Ron Toelke who provided many pictures from his private collection; Terry Moss of Museum Replicas Limited; Peter Harrington and Robert Kenny of the Anne S. K. Brown Military Collection, Brown University Library.

PICTURE CREDITS

The source of each picture used in this book is listed below, by page. When a number of pictures appear on a page, the sources are separated by semi-colons and listed as they appear on the page from left to right and from top to bottom. A number of sources are in shortened form; for the full name, see the list below.

LC—Library of Congress • NA—National Archives • DoF—Department of Defense • CMH—United States Army Center of Military History • NPS—National Park Service • ILN Picture Library—The Illustrated London News Picture Library • Anne S. K. Brown—Anne S. K. Brown Military Collection, Brown University Library.

TITLE PAGE: 2 SuperStock **3** courtesy Ron Toelke, *The Complete Encyclopedia of Illustration,* J.G. Heck, 1851.

TABLE OF CONTENTS: 5 All courtesy Ron Toelke, hand-colored uniform plates of 19th century French military uniforms, illustrated by H. Large, ca. 1895.

INTRODUCTION: 6 MPI Archives; H. Charles McBarron/CMH **7** NA; NA **8** DoF; United Nations.

MAP SECTION: 14-15 map by Ron Toelke, cartographer **16** all maps by Ron Toelke, cartographer **17** all maps by Ron Toelke, cartographer.

A: 18 U.S. Navy **19 AIRCRAFT FEATURE PAGE:** LC; U.S. Airforce; U.S. Airforce; U.S. Airforce **20** SuperStock **21** H. Charles McBarron/CMH; Don Troiani/NPS **22 ARMOR FEATURE PAGE:** courtesy Museum Replicas Limited; courtesy Museum Replicas Limited; DoF; courtesy Ron Toelke, hand-colored uniform plates of 19th century French military uniforms, illustrated by H. Large, ca. 1895 **23** NA; DoF **24 ARTILLERY FEATURE PAGE:** SuperStock; LC; DoF; Don Troiani/NPS **25** DoF.

B: 26 DoF **27** courtesy Ron Toelke, *Days of Glory,* Frederic Villiers, G.H. Doran, NY 1920 **28** NPS, Museum Management Program and Guilford Courthouse National Military Park, photo by Khaled Bassim; NA **29** courtesy Ron Toelke, *The Wonder Book of Soldiers,* edited by Harry Golding, F.A. Stockes Co., NY, 1913 **30 BOW & ARROW FEATURE PAGE:** LC; © Asian Art & Archaeology, Inc./Corbis; courtesy Ron Toelke, from a German pamphlet titled "Schilderung Und Abbildung Der Merkwürdigsten Russischen Volkerschaften welch in dem jetzigen Kriege gegen Frankreich Kampfen," J.A. Bergk und C.O.H. Geissler, Leipzig, 1807; © Bettmann/Corbis **31** © Corel Corporation; LC **32** SuperStock; © Werner Forman/Art Resource, NY.

C: 33 Steve Vidler/SuperStock **34 CAVALRY FEATURE PAGE:** ILN Picture Library; NPS; courtesy Ron Toelke, *The Wonder Book of Soldiers* **35** SuperStock; Dover Publications **36 CHEMICAL & BIOLOGICAL WEAPONS FEATURE PAGE:** NA; DoF;

Corp. **37** DoF; LC **38 COMMUNICATIONS FEATURE PAGE:** SuperStock; Anne S. K. Brown; Don Troiani/NPS; Art Explosion, Nova Development Corp.; DoF; Art Explosion, Nova Development Corp. **39** courtesy Ron Toelke, *The Wonder Book of Soldiers* **40** courtesy Museum Replicas Limited; Christie's Images/SuperStock.

E: 41 NA **42 EDGED WEAPONS FEATURE PAGE:** courtesy Museum Replicas Limited; LC; Art Explosion, Nova Development Corp.; courtesy Museum Replicas Limited **43** SuperStock **44 EXPLOSIVES FEATURE PAGE:** courtesy Ron Toelke, *Harper's Weekly,* 1864; NA; DoF; LC; DoF.

F: 45 LC **46 FIREARMS FEATURE PAGE:** Art Explosion, Nova Development Corp.; Art Explosion, Nova Development Corp.; DoF; NPS; NPS; NPS **47** U.S. Marine Corps History Center; *Bannerman Catalog of Military Goods,* DBI Books, Northfield, IL, 1980 **48 FLAGS FEATURE PAGE:** LC; SuperStock; courtesy Ron Toelke, German book titled *Der Alte Fritz in 50 Bildern für Jung und Alte;* Indochina Archives, Berkeley; MPI Archives **49** Anne S. K. Brown; ILN Picture Library **50 FORTIFICATIONS FEATURE PAGE:** MPI Archives; H. Charles McBarron/CMH; LC **51** courtesy Ron Toelke, *Der Alte Fritz in 50 Bildern für Jung und Alte;* Dover Publications **52** courtesy Ron Toelke, *The History of a Bearskin,* Jules De Marthold, illustrated by J.O.B. Dodd, Mead & Company, NY, 1893; National Gallery of Canada, Ottawa.

G: 53 MPI Archives **54** NA; NA **55** H. Charles McBarron/CMH; © Burstein Collection/Corbis **56** Photographer, Jeremy Andrew Murray for MPI **57** NA; Don Troiani/NPS **58** Dover Publications; NA.

H: 59 © Sandro Vannini/Corbis **60** DoF **61 HORSE FEATURE PAGE:** LC; Christie's Images/SuperStock; LC; NA; Culver Pictures, Inc./SuperStock **62** NA; DoF **63** © Archivo Iconografico, S.A./Corbis.

I: 64 DoF **65** LC; NA **66 INFANTRY FEATURE PAGE:** MPI Archives; CMH; DoF; Don Troiani/NPS **67** LC; Iranian publication.

J-K: 68 Anne S. K. Brown **69** courtesy Ron Toelke, *The History of Our Country,* Vol. 1, Edward S. Ellis, H.W. Knight, NY, 1900; NPS, Museum Management Program and Valley Forge National Historical Park, photo by Carol Highsmith/Khaled Bassim **70** courtesy Museum Replicas Limited; courtesy Museum Replicas Limited; courtesy Museum Replicas Limited; SuperStock **71** NA.

L: 72 LC **73** Anne S. K. Brown.

M: 74 DoF **75 MACHINE GUN FEATURE PAGE:** Old Salem Restoration, Winston-Salem, N.C.; NA; DoF; Art Explosion, Nova Development Corp **76 MEDALS, AWARDS, HONORS FEATURE PAGE:** Institute of Heraldry; H. Charles McBarron/CMH; MPI Archives; © Hulton-Deutsch Collection/Corbis; © Peter Russell, The Military Picture Library/Corbis; DoF **77** DoF; courtesy Museum Replicas Limited **78 MEDICAL TREATMENT FEATURE PAGE:** LC; MPI Archives; Heustis Medical Museum; Don Troiani/NPS. **79** © Corel Corporation; Anne S. K. Brown **80** © Bettmann/Corbis; CMH **81 MISSILES, SATELLITES FEATURE PAGE:** Anne S. K. Brown; Lockheed

Martin; DoF; DoF; DoF **82** AP; Art Explosion, Nova Development Corp. **83** Don Troiani/NPS.

N-O: 84 Peter Willi/SuperStock **85** © Nik Wheeler/Corbis; DoF; DoF **86** LC.

P: 87 Bison Picture Library **88** *Bannerman Catalog of Military Goods;* SuperStock **89 PISTOL FEATURE PAGE:** *Bannerman Catalog of Military Goods;* © Ali Meyer/Corbis; Private collection; DoF; DoF **90** courtesy Museum Replicas Limited; courtesy Museum Replicas Limited; AKG London/Peter Connolly **91 PRISONERS OF WAR FEATURE PAGE:** LC; Anne S. K. Brown; NA; CMH; ILN Picture Library **92 PROJECTILES AND AMMUNITION FEATURE PAGE:** Anne S. K. Brown; NA; NPS, Museum Management Program and Valley Forge National Historical Park, photo by Carol Highsmith and Khaled Bassim; © Gregory Marx, Frontier Americana; cannonball and shell, NPS, Museum Management Program and Valley Forge National Historical Park, photo by Carol Highsmith and Khaled Bassim **93** Hermitage Museum, St. Petersburg, Russia/SuperStock.

R: 94 LC **95** SuperStock; Springfield Armory National Historic Site **96** ILN Picture Library; © Rosenthal Art Slides, Philadelphia Museum of Art.

S: 97 Culver Pictures, Inc./SuperStock **98** LC; LC **99** LC; courtesy Museum Replicas Limited; Dover Publications **100** DoF; Musee Nat. du Chateau de Malmaison, Rueil-Malmaison/Lauros-Giraudon, Paris/SuperStock **101** LC **102 SPIES, ESPIONAGE FEATURE PAGE:** LC; DoF; NA; LC; LC **103** LC; LC **104 SUBMARINES FEATURE PAGE:** courtesy Ron Toelke, *Der Bau von Unterseebooten auf der Germaniawerft,* H Techel, J.E. Lehmanns, Munich, 1922; LC; LC; LC; DoF **105** LC; DoF.

T-U: 106 © Richard Luce **107 TANK FEATURE PAGE:** ILN Picture Library; LC; ILN Picture Library; DoF **108** DoF; DoF; LC.

109 UNIFORMS FEATURE PAGE: courtesy Ron Toelke, from a German pamphlet titled "Schilderung Und Abbildung Der Merkwürdigsten Russischen Volkerschaften welch in dem jetzigen Kriege gegen Frankreich Kampfen," J.A. Bergk und C.O.H. Geissler, Leipzig, 1807; CMH; Art Explosion, Nova Development Corp.; DoF; LC.

V-Z: 110 LC **111** DoF; LC **112** DoF; U.S. Senate **113 WARSHIPS FEATURE PAGE:** LC; © Archivo Iconographico, S.A./Corbis; Anne S. K. Brown; Anne S. K. Brown; © Corbis **114** NA **115 WOMAN AT WAR FEATURE:** LC; NA; LC; courtesy Ron Toelke, hand-colored uniform plates of 19th century French military uniforms, illustrated by H. Large, ca. 1895; DoF; ILN Picture Library **116** NA; CMH **117** ILN Picture Library.

DICTIONARY OF MILITARY LEADERS: 118 *The Gallery of Portraits,* Charles Knight, Pall-Mall East, 1833; *The American Revolution,* by John Fiske; *The Gallery of Portraits* **119** *The Gallery of Portraits;* Independence National Historical Park; *The Gallery of Portraits;* NA **120** *The Gallery of Portraits;* NA; MPI Archives; NA **121** LC; LC; LC; U.S. Army.